In Love

Norma Iris Pagan Morales

ISBN 978-1-959895-94-7 (paperback)
ISBN 978-1-959895-93-0 (ebook)

Printed in the United States of America

WESTPOINT
PRINT AND MEDIA

Overview

He stroke his fingers through my hair. The tension between us is rising. He and I both know it's coming. I lean my head towards him, and he does the same. Our lips connect like magnets. The perfect kiss.

After about 8 seconds, I slowly pulled my face away from his face and put it so that my nose would relate to his nose. He looks at me eagerly and smiles.

We stayed in that position for about 5 minutes. Just by that kiss, we know more about each other than we could ever know. We were saving it for when we know we are truly right for each other.

Contents

Chapter 1

Falling in Love

I fell in love with a great guy, or so I thought. I fell in love with Jerry because he believed in me. The way he smiled brightened my day.

I fell in love with the guy that used to call me when I was mad at him and tell me how crazy it was that we had met and that out of all the people in the world it was me he chose. I loved the boy who gave me chills when he said my name.

I fell in love with the way we used to talk and talk for hours and never get bored. I loved him for when he danced around me while I was making food for us. I loved his hugs and the warmth I felt. One time we watched a Disney movie with the blanket up to our necks and the biggest smile on my face.

Every time there was a funny part, we would throw our heads back in laughter and then our eyes would meet, and the world would stop.

I fell in love with the guy that was there when I thought I wasn't there for myself. I loved him because he made my world better. I fell in love with Jerry.

There was never a time when I couldn't stop smiling while around him. When I was with him the world stopped. We used to hug, and everything was okay for me. I was so happy. While apart from him I felt empty, lost, completely out of it.

Even though I knew he was there, in spirit, I wanted to see his smile 24/7. To have his eyes staring deep into mine was a thrill.

We sometimes had opposing opinions, but our little arguments over who was the best pop singer never got between us. His name being called across the room made my heart skip a few beats.

I would walk past him and his friends at lunch, back and forth, just to see him laughing. I really loved him.

I never noticed how he never acknowledged me when someone else was in the room. I never noticed how he pretended I was a ghost. When his friends made fun of me, he laughed along as if he wasn't texting me, he loved me at the same time.

He hurt my feelings and I came back. I was stupid, but I was in love. He may have used me, but there were little moments that I would always remember that would make me want to just go back. I would do anything just to go back in time, to a month ago, when we were happy.

Have you ever hurt so bad that you just sit and stare into utter nothingness? I loved him. I would've done anything for him, when he asked, I said yes. When he apologized, I didn't think once before taking him back. He made me so happy.

I wasn't going to let me hurt any more than I did. I wanted to smile again, to feel the warmth of his smile as if a thousand suns were shining on us. I didn't want him to leave me, to break me down. But he did, he hurt me.

Now you go ahead and say I'm stupid, but I will always have those happy memories. Seeing him around, still smiling, for a moment I have the same feeling I used to get when I saw him smile. That huge butterfly storm and I smiled for a second too.

Then everything hits me, He's not the one. He doesn't care. I think the hardest thing for me was to realize that I cared so much about him. All I was to him was a girl, who he would take advantage of again, and again.

A girl who cared for him, a girl who made him do stupid things, like a slow dance. I was there for him, I listened to all his problems, I comforted him. No other girl ever did that, so why would he leave me for them? What was so wrong with me? He left me.

It always felt like he loved me, I was so blinded. I wish he had just the tiniest bit of love for me. I deserve a guy who loves me, a guy who sees me and can't take his eyes off me. I want that, I really wanted that with Jerry.

It kills me to think that I will never have that with him. I will never be loved by him. It hurts so much to know that what you really want, more than anything else in the world, you can't have.

I couldn't stop imagining the future. I wanted to go head in and never come out again. I wanted the world to stop spinning. I just wanted him and me, alone, yet together. I believe that some things we did weren't fake, I believe that sometimes he did like running around.

I wanted to think that he went home and thought about me for hours. Then again, I believe he held me in his arms and counted down the seconds until we parted.

I think I saw him in a different light, one where he was my everything. I now realize he is nothing to me, nothing.

Just like I was, and am, nothing to him. Sometimes I used to lie in bed at night and think about him. While being trapped in almost a time warp with him in my mind, I forgot who I was.

Now that we're done, I don't remember who I am. I don't know who I associate with, I don't know what to think, what to do, what to say. It's almost like I thought about his life more than I ever thought about myself.

Sometimes I thought about what I was going to say to him when we were together, everything was staged in my mind. I was ready to play it all out.

I made funny lines and jokes and fell in love with my fairy tales. I fell in love with my version of Jerry.

I made up the ideal guy in my head, what he would do, what we would do. I never thought for a second that that's not what he does, he never went out of his way. I saw things he did and made a fantasy of them.

The perfect story for me. I thought and thought about every perfect thing that could happen, but with the wrong guy. He was merely an object that my mind created into completely different things.

Sometimes, while facing a scary situation, he was there with me. It took me a while, but I realize now that it was just me, talking and doing what I wanted in my mind. I never fell in love with Jerry. I fell in love with happiness.

The situations I made up in my head were all just to make me content. John was just the person who was on the physical side of it. I can be happy, happiness is not within a boy, it's within yourself. What do I think is true happiness, not who.

Chapter 2

The Ribbon

The sun was finally rising, and I was there to watch it rise. The bloody red faded into pink; the pink faded to orange.

Usually something as beautiful as this would be amazing to me, but today I just stared blankly out my window. It's over, even before I can fully wake up my mind is filled with thoughts, it's over.

I'll never be held in his strong arms again. Never feel his warm lips pressed against mine. Never hear him whisper "I love you, so many things I'll miss.

So many memories I hold that are going to burden me and I'm not sure yet whether to regret it all or not. He's the reason I know love. He's the reason for the smile on my face the last few months.

Yet, he's the reason I can't even look at myself in the mirror. He's the reason I lay here watching such wonderful things with lifeless eyes. I'm not sure how to feel, and this is just the very beginning of the day.

My fingers meet my neck as if by instinct to find his necklace. The beloved Virgin Mary I've been carrying around since that cold November day. The little piece of him I carried with me always, as if to show I was his, or was his.

The words hurt even in my mind. Feeling around my skin for it I remember the anger I had had last night and crawled out of bed. I remember ripping it off me and throwing it across the room.

In the faint sunlight I see the little silver piece of metal glinting in the corner next to my dresser. I retrieve it and feeling the cold texture beneath my fingers triggers a hundred memories at once.

I and him together in the woods, sneaking kisses as we threw leaves at each other. One had got caught in my hair and as he gently took it out, he had kissed my forehead.

Then slowly my cheek, down to my neck, then finally right on the Virgin Mary. After that memory flew by the one of him handing me the necklace came to mind. He had put it on me himself and whispered, "You're not allowed to ever take it off. You're mine always."

I clamp my eyes shut and curl up in a ball right on the floor. There's nowhere I can hide when I close my eyes he's there. Him and that beautiful face, beautiful smile, everything.

I'm not sure how much a heart can take before it literally breaks but mine aches so badly, I think I'm going to be sick. I pull myself tighter, gripping onto my legs. The rough rope tying the necklace together digs into my clenched fist. There's nothing left to do but cry, so I do.

I'm not sure when the tears stopped but I didn't hear my family moving around downstairs so it must still be early.

Slowly I lift myself from the floor and lifelessly dress myself. I'm not even sure what I put on, I don't even care anymore, and all I know is that I want to go outside. Now. I can't have this with me anymore.

I told him he could have it back, why should I keep it with me? I silently make my way downstairs and open the door. I don't feel myself doing any of these things, but I must be because I'm suddenly outside standing in the middle of the road.

No cars pass by, no neighbor cat's meow, not even a car alarm in the distance. It must be around five a.m. and I am completely alone.

Just staying away to nowhere I fall to my knees on the wet ground; it must have rained last night. I could care less.

Unclenching my hand, I watch the necklace fall to the ground. I need to realize it's not a part of me anymore. It's just a piece of jewelry sitting in the middle of the road. It doesn't hold the memories, I do.

Behind me is the sound of running feet. He was always a fast runner, light on his feet. They gradually slow as they grow closer.

As he realizes there's a girl in the middle of the road, one who probably looks like a mess right now. One who's heart is completely broken. I look up and feel as if a dagger were just thrust at me.

It just seems so wrong to see him standing there in front of me, a picture of perfection. Even from here I can see his dark eyes, I can imagine the emerald, green lines flashing. What an evil twist of fate that we show up here at the same time.

To my surprise he doesn't turn and run the other direction. Instead, he walks toward me and falls beside me. I can hear his deep breaths and possibly even tears.

"I understand if you can't believe me or don't want to hear it, but I am truly sorry."

The sound of his voice is like poison.

"You're right," I say and stand up. "I don't want to hear it. It kills me to not have you, but you know what, if you'd really cared you would have never done anything to hurt me."

"People make mistakes," he mumbled.

"Yeah, they do Carlos, but everything you've said, wasn't a mistake. It was reality, and if that's who you really are I don't want you anymore. Sorry doesn't change a thing.

It wasn't exactly sorry you were saying when you were breaking my heart." I kicked the ribbon at his knees and turned and walked away.

My hands shook, my head was spinning, and my stomach lurched but there was something inside of me that kept me going. Kept me from doing the easy thing and jumping into his arms, forgiving him for all his wrongs.

Someone stronger inside of me knew that the pain would end, a new day would begin, and something greater would come along one day. Plus, there was something oh so satisfying about leaving him alone in the middle of the street.

I think tonight I'll pray for his misery; I wonder if it'd be wrong to be that selfish. Oh well, not like I was ever that religious in the first place.

Here I am again making my way to the train tracks, my sanctuary. I remember wishing I could leave this town and find new places to go, but right now no other place could make me feel better.

No other place would feel like home. I cut through my little dirty path on the side of the road and I'm there. Almost feeling as though I'm back to normal.

I balance on the hard outer railing, feeling as though I'm back to the beginning of summer. And I know I'm going to be okay.

Chapter 3

Memories

A story cannot be completely true, for the truth is called fact, and fact is boring. To tell my true high school war story I must wrap and fold the truth in overdoing.

Transform monotony and routine into fairytale and adventure. Stories are meant to carry the mind from the usual.

In high school there was one thing that made my mind soar and melted away the troubles of life. There is no emotion in the world such as love.

The story I laid before you is one of struggle and heartbreak, of the fine line between love and hate.

I first met George on one of those perfectly hazy mornings where the horizon is lost in fog. Where the place land meets sky is nothing more than a silver sliver.

We spent the boat ride talking, wind in our hair and smiles on our faces. I was young and trapped and he was a free spirit.

He was like no one I had ever met, completely aware of himself with no regard to the thoughts of others, and I was jealous.

All my life I had worried about other opinions, based my interests on what I thought they would accept. I hid my true self and masked it with what I felt others wanted. George, however, seemed to act against the masses.

There was an instant magnetism between us. We were opposites yet, we fit as if created specifically for the other.

His weaknesses were my strengths and what I lacked he possessed in excess. He took my hand, his eyes burning into mine and promised "no matter what, I'll make this work."

He kept his promise. We spent every waking moment in each other's arms and for a time, life was perfect. He was my best friend, my mentor, my hero, and my therapist. He was my first love.

Love, it is a small simple word. A word that holds the indescribable emotion of countless sweethearts that came before, of the endless stream that will follow.

Looking at him, being with him, I felt undying admiration, the utter infatuation, the complete serenity of every love that ever was. Sometimes I felt I might burst with emotion and the memories of my heart would illuminate the night such as no star ever could.

I honestly believed my soul had found its match and we would float through life to our ever after hand in hand.

Naive, I know but my heart was content. On a humid summer afternoon, my world, the one I had grown so accustomed to, dropped out from underneath me.

George stood at my door disturbed and dripping with sweat, tears and guilt. My heart dropped to my feet.

With one glance, I knew my life would never be the same. I asked what was wrong. He shook his head and with a mournful sigh muttered, barely audible, "I can't do this."

He turned quickly and was gone. I stared after him for a moment frozen in fear, and shock. I didn't even realize my feet were moving until I noticed houses and trees blur past. I was running, desperately trying to catch what I had already lost.

When I found him, he was under a canopy of trees. Sun streaming on his face cradling magnitude of the moment.

It had been too long, we were too young, were the excuses he gave me. I never knew love had a time limit.

He pulled me in for one last embrace and we stood there, on the gravel path, beneath the trees and the sunlight. I never wanted to let go.

I left him there and walked home alone. The same path that had taken seconds before lay ahead of me never-ending.

I finally reached my room and collapsed on my floor and did not move for days. Every ounce of strength was drained.

For weeks I was unable to sleep or eat. I didn't want to see or speak to anyone. The pain was unbearable. I slowly became numb. I was crushed under the weight of my thoughts and memories.

It was a paralyzing sadness that gripped my heart and made me believe I was nothing. I hated him for doing what he did.

I wanted to go back in time and change things, make things better. Mend the gaps that had grown between us and live in happiness again.

I wanted him to care, to miss me, to want me. Most of all I hated myself. Hated myself for caring, for not being what he wanted, for losing him.

I believed for a long time that I needed him to be happy. That without him I was nothing.

Slowly I came to realize that fighting a losing battle was pointless. That what had happened can never be erased.

I began to live again. He opened my eyes in more ways than one. Because of him I no longer take the little things for granted.

Every moment is a gift to be cherished and not one second should ever be wasted. Now, I view autumn leaves spiraling down with awe and soaking up the rays of the burning sun eagerly.

I listen to the people around me and realize each has a story, a history that I will never understand.

He taught me that who I am is all I ever need to be, and changing for anyone else is pointless. I was no longer mourning his loss.

He was my first love but there will be more to come. I am who I am because of my past.

Every day builds upon the experiences of the last. Looking back now with tear-filled eyes a smile dances across my lips. For I know the heartbreak was worth the memories.

Chapter 4

Kissing Me Deeply

I just want you to walk away. The knives are still on my back. But I don't care. People like you were put on this earth for a reason. My feet hit the ground with my tears, all in time with the music. How does this make you feel?

I feel your eyes on the back of my head. I turn to look at you. The heat waves coming up from the ground make it hard to see you.

I do see you. I look in your eyes like it were another day. But today I see it differently than yesterday.

Today I see that you lied to me. But why? You're hurting now. All because of this lie you just told me. I realize it's a lie. I start walking back to you. You look nervous, but you stay where you are. I am six inches from you.

I can hear your heart beat harder and harder. I reach my hand up under your hair, intertwine my fingers with it, then pull you into me. Our lips touch. You gasp. You hesitate. Now, all is forgotten.

You throw your arms over my shoulders and play with the small hairs on the back of my neck. Our hearts beat together. I feel your tears run down my face. I'm scared of what is running through your head, but I only kiss you harder. I kiss you harder. I'm not going anywhere.

Chapter 5

My Best Friend

My best friend wasn't a girl. Nope, he wasn't just a boy either. He was my ex-boyfriend.

Jose and I were together for 3 months before I noticed that I had no interest in him anymore. I was bored with him. It wasn't that I didn't like him anymore. I just wanted to change. I wanted something new. So, I broke up with him.

It wasn't until school was out that I realized how much I was going to miss him. Our relationship was perfect.

We got along so well that when he fought it was over stupid things like if he knew my birthday or what color my eyes are.

When I ended it, things changed…

We talk just as much as we had when were dating, but he never smiled when he was around me. We talked on the phone and texted more than ever, but Jose just wasn't happy.

I told him everything. He liked to tell me that he knew me better than I knew myself. I was beginning to believe him. I felt like I knew nothing about him, like he was a stranger.

When we talked, he still told me he loved me in the only-as-a-friend-way. Little did he know, every time he said that it broke my heart a little more. I watched him talk to other girls. I watched him look at them. Worst of all, I watched him let them take my place.

As he talked to them, he smiled and opened his eyes wide as if he were looking at a legendary piece of art. He used to do that with me; he used to look at me like I was the Mona Lisa.

Now, he looks at me like I'm his mom. Well, not exactly his mom, but more like a friend who he would never be attracted to.

Just like one of the guys. I still looked at Jose like he was an angel. Jose's eyes were as blue as the ocean. When he smiled, he lit up the room, and together we were perfect. Jose seemed to think otherwise.

Jose had forced me to go to a party with him tonight. He didn't want to look weird showing up alone. So, I was forced to go to a party with the guy I love and watch him talk to other girls and flirt.

Just then, he turned to me and said, "Hey Leah? Do you want to get going? I'm bored." He was saying this to me, the girl he was talking to was jealous.

Jealous of me, his pathetic ex-girlfriend. I nodded, afraid that if I talked, I would burst into tears.

As we walked out to his car, he put his arm around me and said, "You know how much I love you, Leah? You're the best friend I could ask for.

You come to boring parties with me every Friday! You know you don't have to, right? Why don't you go hang out with your other friends? Oh no, I didn't mean that to be mean.

I want you here, really, I do." It confirmed my worst fear. I started to cry. It wasn't that he hadn't seen me cry before he had. Plenty of times, almost too many times. I stopped walking; he turned to look at me, "What Leah? What's wrong?"

"Nothing Jose. It's nothing!" I squeaked out of my throat; I sounded like a dying frog.

"Nothing, really Leah? That doesn't seem like nothing to me." I tried to smile but despite my efforts it wasn't going to happen.

I just couldn't smile no matter how hard I tried.

"Well, I think nothing is kind of an understatement but it's nothing you can help me with…" he grabbed my chin before I could finish.

"What are you doing?" I was confused; didn't he know I was crying because I still loved him?

"This…" he said and then kissed me. This was the best kiss I'd had; it was perfect. He had improved since the last time we kissed.

This was only going to make things harder. If he kissed me and didn't feel the spark, he would go back to those other girls.

He would leave me here, crying by myself. It was the one kiss that could make or break our relationship forever.

As I realized this, I cried harder. "Leah, stop. That was supposed to make you happy. Did I do something wrong?" He frowned and I looked down at my feet. I just wanted to break down, fall into his arms, and cry my little heart out.

"No, you didn't do anything wrong. I did. I wasn't honest with you. I never told you that I'm still in love with you.

I never really stopped being in love with you. My heart has been yours since the day we met and it doesn't matter if you want it, my heart will always be yours, Jose.

The reason why I'm crying is that I know your heart will never belong to me again no matter how much I want it.

I ruined it the day I broke up with you." His eyes watered. Maybe I wasn't the only one who felt this way?

"Leah, you broke up with me when you did that, I figured you were over me. I never got over you."

My heart dropped into my stomach as if I were riding a roller coaster, adrenaline pumped in my veins. Jose still loved me.

"Did you feel it? I did." He cocked his head to the right; his eyes glazed over in confusion.

"What are you talking about Leah? Did I feel what?" I laughed at his confusion.

"The spark. When you kissed me, it sparked." I was worried he was going to say no.

"Nope, I didn't." My heart came up into my throat. Oh no, I was going to cry again. I tried to read his face was he smiling, that smile turned into a laugh.

Is this all a joke? Does he get amusement out of breaking girls hearts? "I felt fireworks." His smile grew to the size of five-year-olds on Christmas morning. I hit him and smiled.

"Not funny Jose, not funny!" His smile faded.

"Sorry, it was just so easy." He paused and his eyes did thing where I could see him thinking about what to say.

"Leah, this doesn't we are back together, you know that right? How can I trust you not break my heart just like you did last time."

This was going to be harder than I thought. He started to walk away, regretting what he had just done. I walked to his side and grabbed his hand to stop him from leaving me here.

"Now I know how it is without you, now I know that I can't love anyone but you. I love you Jose and I need you to love me back. Then before I knew it our lips were tangled. That was the best answer he could have possible said.

Chapter 6

The Concert

I comb my hair just the perfect way to "kill all the ladies." I put on my checkered earrings, matching shoes, and belt, as well as my favorite black band t-shirt.

Still standing in my room, I pull the concert tickets out of my back pocket and smile as I look at the words "Row 2 Seat 1" emblazed across the front of the ticket.

I still can't believe I was able to get tickets within ten rows of the stage. I finally glance in the mirror one last time before I exit my bedroom.

"Hey, Matt, where are you going?" my roommate asks me curiously when he sees me walking out of our apartment.

"The Eagles are playing tonight, man, didn't I tell you? I got insane tickets! Two rows from the front! I'm so stoked!"

"Have fun!" he encourages me as I depart from our room. I walk outside of the apartment building into the warm evening air. The sun is just beginning to set, and the sky is a fiery red orange.

I reach to my back pocket just to make sure the tickets are still there. I'm so paranoid about misplacing them that I constantly must check that they are still nestled safely in my jeans.

I walk to my 1992 yellow Jeep Wrangler and hop in, trying to rush so as not be late to the concert.

I sped through the busy streets to the stadium where the concert is being held. I get out of the car, lock the door, and instinctively reach to my back pocket.

Yep. Still there. I met up with all my best friends in the parking lot outside of the stadium.

"Hey, what's up, man? Excited?! This concert is going to be so bad!" I exclaim to my friend Darrel, standing on the outside of the group.

"I know, dude!" he replies as he pulls out his ticket and shakes it triumphantly in the air, almost as if he won the ticket in a crazy competition.

After greeting all my friends, we all proceed to enter the arena, anticipating the time of our lives.

We wander through the corridors, trying to find our seats. Finally spotting them after a long ten minutes of extremely crowded hallways and rude fans, we sit down and take in the view.

Thousands of people are sitting in the seats waiting to see the Eagles perform. Flashing cameras are going off in every direction I turn, and loud screams are continuously being head all around us.

The stage is filled with people setting up equipment and tuning instruments. There is a huge screen behind the stage to allow people who aren't as fortunate as us to see.

All the screaming lights and fans seem unreal, as if I was in a dream. Nothing like this ever occurs in real life, for everything as breathtaking as this only happens in movies.

I continued to look around when I saw her. The most beautiful woman I've ever seen.

Her hair is a dusty brown, almost the color of chocolate. It's curly, filled with pizza, late nights at Starbucks, jazz music, and bounce, when she walks of course.

Her eyes are the color of sparkling water in the light of the stadium. Her beauty radiates from her like moonlight on a serene, glassy pond, while her high cheek bones make her seem very proper.

Her thin body is covered with a knee-length black and white, green trimmed dress. I don't know what draws me to her, but suddenly Darrell yanks me back to my seat.

"Dude, what are you doing?" he curiously asks me. I shook my head, coming out of my daze.

"Sorry, dude, I don't know what came over me," even though I knew exactly what had happened.

Apparently, I had walked out of my seat and began to float towards her. My heart ran away from my body, not even thinking about what it was doing.

I feel drawn to her, almost as if she and I are magnets. I feel lost in the massive stadium, for she is the only person I see.

She laughs and flips her hair behind her shoulder. My heart skips a beat. I quickly look around her, trying to catch a glance of the people she's with, hoping no man escorts her. I sigh with relief as I see only girls.

Being in full consciousness now, I start to leave my seat to introduce myself when suddenly, the lights dim, making me stop on my tracks.

Spotlights shine while slow music, which gets increasingly louder, begins to play as the Eagles make their dramatic entrance from underneath the stage. "Can the screaming get any louder?"

I laugh to myself. I turn around and head back to my seat, determined to talk to this beautiful woman before I leave.

The Eagles break into their first song, "Tequila Sunrise," and all my friends start to noisily sing along. I try to have fun and pay attention to the music, but I can't stop thinking about the woman I saw.

I keep nervously glancing at her during the concert, growing more and more anxious about talking to her.

The concert proceeds with my favorite songs playing while I am distracted by the girl ten rows behind me.

"What am I doing?" I ask myself. "You're missing this once-in-a-lifetime concert because of some girl you've never even met."

I try to pay more attention to the music, but it seems distant, far away. It's always been my dream to get this close to any band.

Now that I'm finally here, I can't even focus. On the other hand, no woman has ever made me feel this way before.

I never thought I would see someone and know they're for me. But what is love at first sight? It's a fairy tale! But I really want to meet her! "Be a man!"

I finally made up my mind. "I'm going to talk to her!" I command myself as I leave my seat, hardly realizing my life is about to change forever.

I clumsily left my seat, despite Darrell's words of repercussion. The music is blocked out of my head.

Everything else is a whirl to me, for my eyes only fall upon her. I realize as I am walking that I have my ticket in my hand, which is strange because I thought I put it in my pocket.

I finally completed the ten-mile journey to the twelfth row. My heart is beating faster than a rocket ship.

I carefully made my way towards her, having to focus on each foot as it takes a step, left foot, right foot, left foot, right foot. I went up to her seat and almost forget how to breathe.

"Hey! I saw you in the opening of the concert and I just wanted to meet you!" I nervously tell her as I drop my ticket. She picks it up for me and with a smile, hands it back.

"I'm Sharon," she replies. Her voice sounds like the Hallelujah chorus being sung by thousands of angels.

I reach out to take it back, but we are both frozen to our spots smiling, with our hands still on the ticket.

Chapter 7

My Life Changed

The date was May 4, 2023. May 4th was the day my life changed. She found out she had Acute Lymphoblastic Leukemia.

My first day of my junior year of high school I had AP Chemistry first and second period.

All I could think when I walked into the lab was how am I going to stay awake? I saw the teacher standing by the door and walked over to her.

"Name?" She asked with an annoyed tone.

"Johnny." I said.

"Johnny, do you have a last name?"

"Rivers."

"I'm not kidding. Give me your last name."

"I'm not kidding. My name is Johnny Rivers."

It took her a moment to check the list and check off my name. She then told me, "See the girl with the blonde hair? That's your lab partner for the rest of the year. No substitutions or swaps."

"Alrighty." I said and sulked off to meet my lab partner for the rest of the year, no substitutions, or swaps. I sat down next to my new lab partner.

"Hi, I guess you're my lab partner for the rest of the year, no substitutions or swaps." She said with a smile.

"Hi. My name's Johnny."

"Your name is Johnny?" She asked with disbelief.

"Yes."

She smiled and laughed. "Well, my name's Emma Craig. I moved here from Bath, England a few weeks ago.

I came from a public school in Bath, and I have no clue if I'm going to be able to keep up."

"Well Emma, if you ever need help you know where to find me." We both smiled and began to listen to the lecture.

When Mrs. Bingham finally let us loose with the Brunson burners and extremely dangerous chemicals it was chaos.

The table next to us managed to melt the glass beaker spilling all the contents onto the table leaving a small cat sized hole in the lab table.

The table behind us exploded the contents of their beaker everywhere burning multiple innocent bystanders. We weren't doing too well ourselves.

Emma had beautiful long blonde hair and she forgot to tie it back before we started. About five minutes into our experiment, I looked over and her hair was sizzling and smoking. The smell of her burning hair was overwhelming.

"Emma." I said.

"What?!" She cried. We were both becoming flustered with the assignment.

"Emma!"

"What! Johnny?"

"Your hair!"

"My hair? Oh God." She sprayed her hair down with the water that was sitting on our lab table for events such as this.

"Miss. Craig, I see that you did not follow one of my rules. Do you know what the penalty is for not following my rules?"

"Yes, Mrs. Bingham." Emma said. People all around Emma and I began to snicker.

"And what would that be?" She asked Emma a cruel smile beginning to form on her face.

"I am banned from the lab for the rest of the semester." I couldn't let Emma fail.

"Mrs. Bingham, I distracted Emma and she forgot to pull her hair back." I told Mrs. Bingham.

"Alright, Mr. Bond, detention for a month, Mondays, Wednesdays, and Fridays. I'll be seeing you after school today to start your detentions." She told me.

"Yes, Mrs. Bingham."

"Oh, Emma, next time, I will kick you out of my class." She chastised Emma and returned to the front of the room.

When Mrs. Bingham's back was turned Emma whispered to me. "You didn't need to do that. It was all my fault. I'm lucky I didn't lose all my hair. It's a good thing that this happened.

I've been meaning to get my hair cut short for such a long time. This was the extra push I needed." She told me in a rush of words. I had a hard time following her. "Well if it counts, I like your hair long." I told Emma. I hoped I hadn't freaked her out.

I'd only known her for an hour and a half, and I was already giving her creepy complements.

"Thanks, I'll take that into consideration." She smiled and returned to her lab report.

The bell rang a half an hour later and we packed up. I walked her to her locker. I watched her try to pull her books off the top shelf of her locker. She was up on her tiptoes.

I reached up to help her and everything on the top shelf fell to the floor. I quickly stooped to the ground and started to collect her things.

"Calm down. I'm perfectly able bodied and capable of picking up my own books." She laughed and took her pink notebook from me.

She came a step closer, her hair brushed against my cheek, and she whispered in my ear 'thank you' and hurried off to her next class.

I was stunned and shocked. My heart pounded. My palms began to sweat, and the bell rang. I was late for the third class of my junior year.

I couldn't believe that I could have so much homework the first day of school. It was crazy. I slowly walked back to my locker and put what I needed to bring home into my backpack.

There was no need to hurry, I wasn't going anywhere any time soon. I could sense that somebody was behind me. I turned around to see Emma's beautiful smile and golden hair.

"I just wanted to thank you again for covering for me in chem. class today. Before you go report to detention, I owe you big time."

She smiled, kissed me on the cheek, and went to her locker to get ready to go home. I was beginning to wonder if Emma had this effect on all guys or if it was just me.

The next morning, I couldn't get to chem. class quick enough. Emma walked in ten minutes later with her hair pulled back into a low ponytail with a ribbon.

It was almost like she was mocking Mrs. Bingham. She sat down next to me, my non-substitutable or swappable lab partner.

I could never imagine substituting or swapping Emma for another partner. I hoped she felt the same way.

"I see you remembered to tie your hair back." I said, half laughing.

"Yes, I did." She smiled.

"Your hair looks nice today." I told her.

"Thank you, Johnny." She said to me and began to work on our newest lab assignment.

Three broken glasses and two hours later we had successfully completed the experiment and lab papers.

Mrs. Bingham came around to our table and looked impressed. She passed by without saying a word. Emma and I hi fived when she was over evaluating some other kid's experiment. This little ritual of chemistry class went on for months.

After I finished my detentions, I'd go over to her house, and we would study. Her mom would make dinner and ask the both of us how our days went. It was the same old answer every day.

One day Emma was showing me this amazing pianist on YouTube, and we eventually ended up on his Myspace.

We scrolled down through his comments and saw this Chris Townsend kid. Emma clicked on his name, and it brought us to his page. The first song on his play list off his CD was Stay Positive. We listened to it for a bit. The song was amazing and beautiful.

Emma turned to me and said that this would be our song. She also told me that every time we heard this song, we would think of each other. How could I disagree with her?

The last week of Christmas vacation I finally worked up enough courage to formally ask Emma out. We had gone to many movies and the Christmas Dance together just as very good friends.

We weren't officially "going out" yet. We were sitting in her room reviewing for mid-terms.

"Emma." I called over to her.

"Yes, Johnny?"

"I was wondering if you would like to go ice skating with me tonight."

"Like a date?" She asked, turning around in her desk chair to face me.

"Yes."

"I'd love to." She smiled and came over to me and kissed me on the lips.

There was an outdoor ice rink set up for the weekend at the museum in our town. I decided to take Emma there.

Later that day I picked Emma up at her house. She came down the stairs in an adorable blue jacket and white knit scarf, hat, and gloves combo. We had a great time.

May first came and went without a glitch. The next day I got to chemistry and Emma was not in her seat. I worried the whole entire day. After school I stopped by her house and rang the bell.

Emma answered the door and told me to come in. She took me up to her room and told me to sit down. I did what she said. She did not look like she wanted to be disobeyed.

"Johnny, I went to the doctor today." She told me, sitting down next to me.

"And?" I asked trying to prompt her.

"They found something strange in my blood work. Something not good. They say that I have Acute Lymphoblastic Leukemia. They need to do more blood work but-" I cut her off.

"You have cancer?" I asked.

Emma began to cry. "Yes, I have cancer." She said matter of factly.

"You have cancer?" I said again.

"Yes, James I have cancer. There is nothing I can do about it but accept the fact that I have cancer and start an extremely aggressive chemo. regimen and hope it works."

"Are you going to lose your hair?" I asked her.

"Yeah. I guess I'm going to get that short haircut that I've been wanting." She laughed.

"Are you going to live?"

"They say I will since I caught it so soon. There is an 85% survival rate."

"There is still 15%."

"I know. I'm going to kick that 15% in the butt and make it wish it never thought of saying I was going to die."

"Are you afraid?"

"I'm very scared. Are you afraid?"

"I think I'm even more scared than you."

In the background I could hear our song playing, Stay Positive, by Chris Townsend. At the same exact moment, we looked at each other and said, 'Stay positive'. That was the last time I saw Emma cry.

As the days rolled along Emma's hair began to fall out. It started in small patches that she could easily hide by combing her hair differently. Eventually the bald patches became too noticeable, and she got her head shaved.

One day after school Emma asked me to let her drive home. I had picked her up that morning and was going to drive her home so we could study but I was too smart to disagree.

She had this determined look on her face, and I wasn't going to stop that. We pulled up at the local barber shop and she said, "I'm tired of my hair, I'm getting it shaved off and you are going to stand there and help me get through it."

We walked into the barber shop, and she told the man at the front desk, "I have cancer and my chemo, is making me go bald. I want you to shave my head."

The man at the front desk looked at her in utter disbelief. She was a paying customer, and he couldn't argue.

He walked her over to one of the chairs. He turned the electric razor on and began to shave what was left of Emma's golden locks.

When the man was done, she looked at herself in the mirror, handed the man a twenty, and walked out of the shop.

I caught up with her at the car. "Do you want me to drive you home?" I asked.

"I think that would be a good idea." We spent the car ride to her house in silence.

When we got back to her house she walked inside, and her mother took one look at Emma's nearly bald head and hugged her.

Her mother did not cry, she only held on to Emma for as long as she possibly could before Emma broke away. Emma's mother kissed her on the head and went back into the kitchen.

The next day when Emma and I walked into school, his jaws dropped. People finally realized what was going on with Emma Morales.

They did not fully understand but they had a better idea now that Emma didn't have hair anymore.

When we walked into chem. Emma walked over to Mrs. Bingham and just stared at her. Mrs. Bingham's jaw dropped, and she never gave Emma any more problems.

Mrs. Bingham just looked at Emma with this pathetic look of sympathy and Emma hated that even more than her constant grief.

May came around and prom fever was in the air. Everybody was buzzing. I decided to ask Emma to the prom.

I walk up to Emma's locker at the end of the day as usual and pulled a single daffodil out of my backpack and asked her to prom. She smiled and kindly accepted the flower and my invitation.

May seventh came rolling around sooner than the both of us could imagine. I picked her up at her house. I watched her come down the stairs in a beautiful corn flower blue silk gown, we stood in front of the mantle in her living room for a quick photo opt, and then we were off to prom.

We danced. We talked to our friends. We ate and we had a good time. The last song of the night was our song. We looked at each other and I held her in my arms.

I whispered in her ear, like she did to me so many days ago, but the words were different. I 'love you', I told her. She looked up at me and said, 'I love you too' and rested her head back on my chest.

That summer her cancer took a turn for the worse. The doctors could not seem to get her into remission.

She lay delicately in her hospital bed covered up to her neck in blankets. She was a thin and tired version of the Emma I met so many months ago.

It was August second. I had just come back from eating in the cafeteria at the hospital.

I sat down on her bed and kissed her head. She looked up at me and smiled.

Her smile was beautiful. She whispered to me, 'I love you'. The monitors went dead. She was gone…

Chapter 8

I Can Dance

The world is dancing around me. The colors are swirling and I'm laughing.

"I've never seen the world like this before." I exclaim, still spinning lightly in a circle.

"Everyone could see the world like that if they spun around enough." He chuckles.

I stop, swaying into his arms. He pushes my hair back. I smile.

"Dance with me." It was sudden. "Dance and see the world as I see it."

His smile vanishes. "I - I don't dance." He moves away, pushing me away from him.

"You don't dance?"

"No."

He asked, "Not once?"

"Never."

"Then do it for me." I take his hand.

"Just one dance. Move with me."

He doesn't smile. "I -"

"For me please!"

"I can't. I don't. Never have. Never will."

My smile vanishes. "Anyone can dance."

"Not me."

"Not even for the one you love?"

He isn't smiling. He doesn't face my eyes. The world stopped and it's colors went gray. His voice was gossamer, a piece of the wind.

"No," Where is the world we were just in? "You...You deserve someone....someone who would...dance for you."

I step back. The world of ours has gone, the vastness of the universe has created itself between us. "No..."

"Yes."

We are now two worlds apart, but I know he must've heard me when I said ....

"I don't want to dance anymore."

Chapter 9

Endless Love

"I love you forever" he says.

"Forever is useless" I mutter.

I stared into his deep eyes. I can tell that he really does love me. Doesn't everyone think this? That they are loved?

"I love you during the spring" he whispers holding me gently.

What about the other seasons? "And the winter".

"How about fall"? I whisper back.

"Forever is forever". He kisses me lightly.

"And summer"? I whisper.

I held him tightly. I don't want his warmth to go away. I know inside that I will be weak without it. He held me for a while, and then said, "I love you during the winter, the fall, the summer, and the spring. No matter what. I'll always be here".

I feel tears coming and I wipe them away making them come faster, harder.

"I want to believe you, I just can't. Babe, I love you, I just don't know about forever. Forever is useless."

I look again into his eyes, and I see comfort.

"I still love you forever" he whispers.

He walks away into the night.

I can still smell his cologne.

Even after his steps.

One, Two, Three.

"And a day", I whisper.

That's when I knew that forever isn't useless because I love him forever, just as much as he loves me.

I ran to him, and I said confidently "I love you forever".

Chapter 10

Prince Charming

When David Maldonado transfers to an all-boys high school, he immediately gets a bad impression of his new destroy, David Maldonado.

Gorgeous, mysterious, and menacing, Ivan is exactly what David doesn't need in his life - or so he thinks...

After causing trouble in his previous high school, David is struggling to adapt to his new environment at Ivory High and to stop living in the shadow of his perfect older brother.

As usual, trouble follows David wherever he goes. Nothing is going well. To make matters worse, he seems to have attracted the attention of The Class Prince, the infamous Ivan Martinez.

But despite their rocky start, David begins to grow feelings for Ivan, discovering a new side of his identity that he never thought to experience.

Chapter 11

Jogging Together

Our daily jog together. At least I like to think of it as our jog. It's not like we run together, but in proximity in separate universes.

It is hard to remember the days when we did not run together. My oval-shaped jogs right behind his treadmill and always keeps up.

It would have been so easy to say hi the first time. But with each passing day, it has gotten harder and harder, and now impossible. We have had occasional looks back and forth, but those were probably coincidences.

Of course, I always look at him. As for the times his glance met mine, perhaps something else called his gaze.

I'm way too shy to budge from my routine to approach confirmed rejection. Why can't he just make the move? I know, that's a funny one. Look at him and then look at me – especially without makeup!

I don't turn red from exercising, but I do blush when I'm nervous or embarrassed. So, my cover story would be that my redness is from my heavy-duty workouts.

After all, I am at the gym. I'm struggling to keep up with myself. My mind is going faster than the external oblique muscle.

My intense fears, my anxious nerves, my taxing concerns, my angry anxieties whirling through my brain. Now I'm dizzy.

Even he has weaknesses. It's not like I think he's perfect or anything. How could he be perfect with shoes that smell like that?

He comes close to perfection. His feet come close to me as he lifts them on the treadmill upwind of my elliptical.

Just as my iPod advances to the next song, a wave of toxic air permeates my nostrils. "Tell me how I'm supposed to breathe with no air? Can't live, can't breathe with no air …

If you weren't here, I just can't breathe. There's no air, no air," sings Jordin Sparks. Whew, how can I breathe in this air?

Deep breath in. Deep breath out. Ahh. How can toxic air be refreshing? But amid these toxins, there is some sweetness. I can just sense it; I have that tingling feeling in my nostrils.

It's hard for me to hold back a little smile. I can't get away from it this time. It draws me closer. The occasional silent connection I have with him is worth the foul air I endure. I must be high on either the stench or endorphins because I don't believe in drugs.

I am exercising longer than usual. I am pumped. I am not getting tired. Exercise is a healthy form of procrastination for what I might do next.

The elliptical bars are sandwiched between my palms and my fingers. I am pushing them with all my strength. Just as I alternately push and pull on the levers left, right, left, right.

My strength to contact him alternates with my fear of rejection. Our closeness has been on a metaphorical treadmill, no matter how hard I try, no matter how fast I run, we don't get any closer.

The counteracting forces of acceptance and rejection are pulling on me equally. I am in equilibrium. I am moving at a constant velocity on the elliptical, but I can't get myself to move toward him.

I try to look cute in my gym clothes, but it's hard. The mirror tells me I look fat and ugly. Those are the only things the mirror ever tells me, besides red hair, freckles, Raggedy Anne.

My pink good-luck sweatband hasn't brought me any luck. I'm going to go buy some new colored ones. I'm getting kind of sick of pink.

People must think I wear the same sweaty headband every day, but I have dozens of them from that sale at Costco. I know that's what he's thinking when he turns around: freak, loser.

Droplets of sweat drip down my face, ravaging my pores and burning the roots of my confidence. But he gives me a feeling all over my body just by looking at him. So, I know it's worth it.

The odor burns my nostrils, but I can't resist. I tiptoe into the hallway outside the men's locker room; one hand holding the heart shaped post-It, the other plugging my nose.

I see them resting on the wooden bench, right where he left them after "our" jog, laces untied and tongues forming obtuse angles.

Why are they here? My hands are shaking, and my legs are trembling, but I bite the corner of my lip and stick the note face up in the heel of his right shoe.

I am leaving the gym and I can't stop thinking about him. Still. I hope he feels the same. But he won't. I hope he will call. But he won't. It's been seven minutes since I put my note in his shoe and put my heart on the waiting list for rejection.

I enter my apartment and begin pacing. It's been an hour and three minutes. I shouldn't have done it. He doesn't like me. It's going to be awkward.

No way. I'm not giving in. I'm not going to change my workout routine. But it will be hard to look at him tomorrow. I hope he saw the note before he put his shoes on. If not, I hope the ink doesn't smear.

There she is. I could set my watch by her if I had one. Same gym. Same time. Same workout. Same as me. She never misses a day. I don't think I ever will either.

My mom and dad are both kind of, I don't want to say chubby, but yeah, they are. I can't let that happen to me. I have another reason too.

My neck always cracks when I turn my head swiftly to check the clock behind me. At first this was a pain, but then I saw her.

When I realized I got to look at her every time I turned to check the time, my neck strain didn't bother me.

I must be discreet. I love looking at her, but I don't want her to know that her beauty keeps me staring.

At least not quite yet. I'm not a stalker, just shy. I want to talk to her. I want to go up to her. But what if she thinks I'm just hitting on her? I'm really interested in knowing her. How is she supposed to tell the difference?

What a cutie. She's just my type: tall, slender, and I can tell her skin is smooth. The cutest freckles.

Milk chocolate eyes. Her gorgeous, wavy red hair is tied back in a ponytail and she wears a pink headband. She must love pink. She should, it's her color. Her hair sways with every step. Thank you, pink headband, not a hair is blocking my view of her face.

What I like most is that she doesn't act like she is beautiful. She doesn't know how nervous she makes me.

She doesn't know the grace she displays. She has a story to tell. I want to hear it. I'm afraid to ask her.

Wimpy, maybe. Intimidated. I feel like I've watched the same Candid Camera episode 5,500 times.

My failed attempt keeps replaying in my head. With every day that I say nothing, she's more and more likely to think I'm either gay or I need a watch.

I want to know her name. Seeing her every day for weeks, I refer to her as Pink Headband. How pathetic. I must know her name.

At least for now, it would be easier to ask the receptionist for Pink Headband's name than to ask her. At least if she refuses, it won't be as humiliating as a no from Pink Headband.

So, I make my way to the desk. I say excuse me to the nerdy girl behind the counter. I have caught her staring at me in the past, but the one time I want her attention, she's preoccupied.

I'm the only person here. The phone is resting comfortably on its hook. But she is talking to someone or something, nonetheless. I sigh.

I'm getting impatient. I feel like I'm hailing a taxi. Waving and waving, and they just drive by. Same with her. I'm waving and that freak seems to be talking to her stapler.

Finally, I got her attention. I ask. She answers. I write "Debbie" on the envelope containing my note to the woman I used to know as Pink Headband. I ask the receptionist to please give it to her.

As I sit on the bench outside the men's locker room, I fight my urge to chicken out and retrieve the envelope.

I escaped into the locker room to take a shower. The hot water is soothing. Shoot! I left my shoes on the bench. Not to worry. Who would want to steal those smelly old things?

Realizing I must have left my cell phone in my car, I get dressed quickly, jump into my shoes, and leave. I don't want to miss her call.

I hate working in this place. Why do I work here? I need out. I need a workout. I'm so funny. I always laugh at my own jokes.

All day I inhale air tainted with the smell of sweat. No, it's not me doing the sweating. Oh, here comes Mr. "I'm so much better than you that I won't respond when you greet me."

I scrunch my nose to push up my glasses, the way I always do when my hands are busy. He's headed right toward me. It seems like he needs to ask me something. This will be my first.

How will he do this and keep his perfect record of never saying a word to me? Of course, it must be so hard to say "good evening" to someone who has just said it to you.

I can feel my nervous twitch starting up again. My top lip is moving diagonally; my invisible enemy has strung a thread through my lip with his needle. I try to yank it in the other direction, back into place, but it won't budge.

The name of the girl in the pink headband? The girl in the pink headband! If she's wearing her pink one today, it must be either Sunday, Monday, Tuesday, Wednesday, Thursday, Friday, or Saturday. Gross.

Apparently, he either doesn't notice or doesn't care. How sweet. For once he is nice and it is hard to hate him. He writes "Debbie" on the envelope and hands it to me. Sure, I'll give it to Debbie, all right.

He heads for the locker room; he is out of sight, but he sure isn't out of my mind. Neither is the favor he asked of me.

He wants me to give the envelope to Debbie. Sure, I will. I'll be as good at giving this to Debbie as he is at responding when I say hello.

Better because now my paper shredder's name is Debbie. Debbie loves envelopes. She'll fall bin over wheels!

Chapter 12

In Class

My eyes scanned the large classroom. There she is. Her long, wavy brown hair was shining in the sunlight coming through the window.

Beautiful. I smiled as I made my way through the cramped space between the tables.

When I got closer, I noticed the book on the chair beside her, saving my seat. She turned around in her chair and, seeing me coming, smiled a huge smile, moved the book onto the table, and cast her gorgeous sky-blue eyes toward the chair.

It was from this that I gave her the nickname, Sky. I know. Original, right? But it suited her, and she loved it. As always, she was wearing the necklace I had made for her birthday last year, which brought out her eyes wonderfully.

"Morning, Gabriel. How was your date?" She waggled her eyebrows up and down a few times. Ugh. Did she have to remind me?

The night before, I had suffered through endless pain and agony on the worst blind date of my life. Because of what she called her "maternal duty" my mother had set me up with the "delightful and charming" Amalia-daughter of my parent's affluent neighbors, Stephen, and Linda Smith.

Amalia was, basically, what every guy, but me apparently, would have wanted in a blind date. She was the blond, leggy, voluptuous, bad-private-school girl type, and to top it all off--captain of the cheerleading team. Can you say cliché?

"Don't ask."

"That bad?"

"She thought Leonardo de Caprio painted the Mona Lisa."

Sky's sweet, lilting laugh filled the space between us. "Ouch."

"Yeah." I sighed. Ouch indeed.

"You'll find someone." She said as Professor Newman began the lecture. I wanted to tell her I already had found someone, she just happened to have a boyfriend and was, apparently, completely oblivious to the fact that I had a Y chromosome.

I had been in love with Sky since I first met her in our psychology class at the beginning of the year. It was her sophomore and my junior year at Rayford Barnes University.

The seat next to mine was the only one not being occupied. She stumbled in at the last minute, her hair sticking up, shoes untied, and loaded down with a monstrous backpack and a stack of books in her hand.

Trying to put the books on the table, she swung her backpack around and brained me in the face. When I woke up, the first thing I saw were those dazzling eyes staring down at me. I was hooked.

Since then, I had been upgraded to best friend status, helping with problems, and giving advice, all the while secretly pining like the hopeless loser I am.

As a best friend should, I learned every possible thing about her. Things not even her boyfriend knew. Like she had been diagnosed with acute lymphoid leukemia when she was ten years old and had a complete remission.

She still slept with her teddy bear, Ernest, that she got for her third birthday. Everything from her favorite color, viridian, the color you would get if you mixed her sky-blue eyes with my dark green ones, to her first kiss, junior year, YMCA parking lot, Redmond Willer, his real name, believe it or not, to the way she liked her jeans to fit, loose in the thigh, low on the hips.

I could tell you anything. I was overjoyed to be her friend, I really was. I just longed for something more. I felt something warm on my hand.

Glancing down, I saw Sky's hand resting on mine, and I felt a jolt of electricity charge through my veins.

"Gabriel?" Professor Newman was right next to my desk, a knowing expression on her face. It was beyond obvious that this wasn't the first time she had tried to get my attention, which probably explained Sky's hand on mine.

Glancing over at her, I could see that she was slightly worried, unlike Professor Newman, who was smirking at me.

She was incredibly young for a professor, probably in her mid-thirties, and wore different rims around her glasses every day.

This was my second semester of psychology with her, and I had never seen her wear the same ones twice. They were all different colors and shapes.

Some had leopard print or rhinestones. It was as if she used them to see inside our heads. She was one person you couldn't keep secrets from, which, I guess, made sense, her being the psychology teacher and all.

Even now, as she looked at me, I could tell she knew how I felt about Sky.

"Sorry, what was that?" I managed, trying to concentrate on talking, rather than the fact that Sky was touching me.

"Your homework, Gabriel." Professor Newman said gently as she rolled her eyes. It was all I could do not to moan out loud when Sky removed her hand so that I could grab my bag.

I fumbled for the right papers and handed them to her, trying out what I hoped was an apologetic smile.

As she took them, she shook her head in a will-he-ever-learn kind of way. Moving to the front of the room, she sighed and ran a hand through her thick, black hair before turning back to face the class.

"Please turn to page 253 in your books and we'll get started." She said calmly. I read the title of the page we were about to study. Social Influences on Love and Mate Selection. No freaking way.

Chapter 13

Mark's Death

His name was Mark Delgado. He prepared his own meals, made his own wine, and polished his own shoes. He was a very independent man.

He was born January 17, 1945, and he grew up in the hard but modest streets of South Side, Brooklyn in the 1950s.

Every moment of his life was life threatening. Condemned with an unknown disease, Mark had great philosophy. "You must dare, to be Great!" He would shout whenever he felt sick.

He worked hard to become successful after the past had escaped him. He was ready for a new life and a new beginning. He was tired.

Mark's strong attitude and personality was the cause of his success. Money was his downfall; he had already reached his peak.

Mark was the conquistador who later lost it all by an act of greed and violence. The longer he was on top, the faster his decline would be.

He lived and begged for some time. Mark lived in the shadows his entire life until he met his wife, Margarita. He knew he had found his guardian angel.

He married her to regain hope. His hope was to be in absolute redemption. His life became unknown and insignificant to the world. Mark was now a husband who had quit his job of corruption and hate.

He never meant to cause any trouble in Brooklyn, his organized crime days were over.

It was July 18, 1968, when Mark Delgado had come out of his shell and like other men, it was the time for a new opportunity.

He had left behind his old house, neighborhood, barbershop and church just to start over.

He moved to Chicago. He was so desperate for a new start. He was eager to get a head start. He picked up the newspaper at the nearest kiosk.

He skipped the sports section and the breaking news section to immediately turn to the employment ad section. His change would begin by changing his career.

His wife, Margarita, would shine light in his world of horror. She helped him gain the confidence he lacked since his early career.

"How much?" Mark asked the clerk in a New York accent.

"Twenty-Five cents." The clerk responded.

As Mark reached into his pocket for a quarter, the clerk stopped him and asked, "You are not from around here... Are Ya?"

"No." Mark responded nervously, afraid that his past came to haunt him.

"Alright then. Sir, you have a good... no, Great Day!"

Mark took his hand out of his right pocket and reached for his wallet. He took out a dollar bill and put it on the stand. "Here you go.

Keep the change and have a great... no, good day!" Mark said, almost mocking the clerk.

The clerk smiled at him. Mark walked away. Mark went to the parking lot by the diner to check if his car was still there. 1958 Chevy Impala, Classic. Seeing that it was still there, he went on looking for the nearest place that was hiring.

He read the whole section boxing in the jobs he was interested in and crossing out the ones he was not.

Out of a total of twenty-three jobs listed, he crossed out twenty-one. Left with two he decided to go with one.

He knew this one was the one. He had a business background and had lots of experience. He thought he was a great salesman and deserved this job.

The place was only a few blocks from where he was, and he decided to call "Al" on a pay phone.

He looked around for the nearest phone available. He spotted one besides the stand he was at earlier. Mark knew better and avoided any conflict with that clerk. He walked around the opposite corner to look for a pay phone.

Urgency took over his thoughts. He promised his wife he would get a job that very day…

Meanwhile, Margarita was planning a congratulatory dinner for him. She thought this dinner would motivate him.

She hadn't been satisfied by her husband since he was diagnosed with the disease. The mixture between his smoking habits and the pollution of New York City have caused consequences.

Margarita saved his life by making him quit smoking. Mark was very determined and with treatment, he would live for more than twenty years.

Although the cancer was asleep, he didn't feel like Margarita deserved a man like him. He was self-centered, he wanted to keep Margarita for his benefit. He was a better man now. Margarita was ready to make this night, a night they shall both remember forever.

Margarita seemed like the perfect wife. She knew how to cook, wash the dishes, and iron. Most importantly, she didn't like arguments.

Her payment was average. Mark would fix himself up for her. Nothing was as ordinary compared to the debt he owed her.

Margarita worked as a secretary at a law firm. She was known in the office by her alias, Margarita "Tabloid" Delgado.

She was given this nickname because she knew everything about everyone in the law firm, and possibly Chicago.

She started to prepare the dinner by greasing a pan with butter and reading from her ingredients. She was making a very boring, average steak and salad dinner.

That dinner was an American style Italian dinner. There was no way that Margarita would ever prepare a meal that came close to the aroma or zest Italians had.

It didn't matter to her as her plan was to obtain some satisfaction. The telephone rang. It was…

Mark had asked pedestrians the location to a near pay phone. They all pointed to the same one.

Mark had no choice but to go to the one by the kiosk. He walked towards the phone. As he approached the stand, he turned his head towards the street to avoid eye contact with the clerk.

Not paying attention to the walk ahead of him, he crashed into a light post. Surprised, Mark looked around to see if anyone was laughing. He saw the smirk on the clerks' face.

"What are you looking at?" he screamed. He repeated the same thing three times, adding slang and he began to swear.

His commotion led to no one. He was just simply looking down screaming towards the pavement. There was something wrong with Mark. He was paranoid. His life in Brooklyn affected his mentality.

Finally realizing that he was making a fool of himself, he looked up and saw no one in the street. The Kiosk was being maintained by the clerk.

He was paying no attention. Mark really felt ignorant at that point and then walked by the phone. He dialed the number to Al's. The phone was ringing and Al himself picked up the phone.

"Al's Major Automobile Emporium, how can I help you?"

"Yes, my name is Mark Delgado, I saw your Ad in the newspaper, and I'm interested in working as a car salesman."

He was very nervous. His voice was not of a salesman and Mark was afraid that he blew it.

"Nice to meet you, Mr. Delgado, all I can say is, you are hired!" Al screamed with extreme over enthusiasm.

"Really?" Marl said, confused.

"Yeah, I'm just happy someone called!"

Mark was very excited, and he jumped for joy. He attempted a heal click but he failed.

It looked like a very ridiculous out of balance jump. This time the clerk saw it and began to laugh uncontrollably. Mark heard his laugh but ignored it.

"Thank you, Mr. Al,"

"Thank you, Mr. Delgado, and you start tomorrow. Also, please call me Al."

"No problem, Thank you Bye"

"Goodbye" Al said.

Mark ran off the telephone. He remembered the clerks laughs. He went up to his stand.

He gave him a big hug. It was uncomfortable because there was three feet of width between him and the other side of the stand.

Mark came back to the telephone and decided to call Margarita.

Now I am hearing the great news about her husband. Margarita was motivated to create the best dinner of his life. She even dressed up sassy for him. The door opened. It was Mark.

Very exhausted from his ride home, Mark told Margarita to get him a drink immediately. No greeting, no kiss, no hello.

"Yes." Margarita said, interrupted by Mark.

"Just give me my wine. I'm not interested." Realizing that Margarita made dinner he said, "Ahh, you made dinner! Good! I'll go upstairs and change…Wait, my drink."

"I will get it" Margarita said doubting whether to congratulate Mark about his day. She decided not to and left.

All she wanted was for her benefit. She just wanted her husband to be excited and lively for tonight.

She went into the kitchen to get the wine from the cellar. She saw that she did not need to go to the basement because the wine bottle was on the dining room table.

She reached into her pocket and added an ingredient to the food and the wine. This secret ingredient was Sildenafil citrate. A solution that would get a man at his peak in no time.

A symptom of his disease consisted of erectile dysfunction. Margarita had begun to show despair. This night might be the night that she would benefit from her marriage.

She walked back to him and handed him the glass. Without saying a word to each other, he snatched the glass from her hand, almost spilling it.

He took a sip and smiled. He ran upstairs. She got herself ready by lighting some candles and heating up the food once more. She waited for her husband to come down.

Margarita heard a weird noise coming from the stairs. Her first thought was that Mark had fallen down the stairs. He was unconscious.

A great shadow emerged over him as the light faded from his face. He was dead. Margarita checked his pulse. She didn't bother trying to resuscitate him. It was over.

She still had no idea what had happened that night or what killed him. She questioned whether it was the fall, or the wine that killed him. She overlooked one detail.

She had killed the man she was guarding over. She lost the man she choose to wed. She betrayed her own light and committed the worst crime of all. She committed deception.

Chapter 14

The Midnight Dance

The stars were shining above us. Each dazzling star was a light on a disco ball that Anibal and I danced under.

The night was dressed in inky black to match my clothes. Anibal and I change direction in and out of the trees to our own beat.

Grass was the perfect dance floor. The softness of it cushioned our steps. Nature was all the music we needed.

The chilling wind was our pipes, seedpods were our maracas, and the pecking of a bird was our drum. The leaves so high on the trees were swaying with us in the wind. This part of the world was meant for us.

How long could this last? A second, a minute, an hour, a day, a lifetime? The crisp air held no answer for us. We just kept weaving back and forth in each other's arms. Time was not our problem, nor was hate, envy or competition. The world for that moment was perfect and could never be duplicated.

Anibal and I were spinning around a rose bush when I heard the crack of a gun and Anibal went down.

I was so confused I didn't know what was happening. Anibal's body fell to the ground as I dropped next to him.

Blood was seeping through his shirt like a raging river. My salty tears mixed with his blood as I sat there gazing into his glassy blue eyes. I laid my head on his chest sobbing when the police sirens could be heard in the distance.

The sirens were getting closer. They could be heard right ahead of us. I lifted my tear-streaked face to meet the officer when I heard a faint sound. I turned my head towards Anibal and then I realized his pale lips were moving.

I fell to my knees at his side listening. Barely louder than the coo of a dove he whispered, "Remember me, Alicia. Remember me and our midnight dance."

Then Anibal left this world. He left me. Left an unfinished dance that could have lasted a lifetime.

Chapter 15

The Moment

I was swinging all alone. I could hear it squeak as I went up and down. A cold breeze ran through my bones as a tear rolled down my face.

As usual I had been thinking about you. You said my name. My swing had almost completely stopped. I was shedding tears constantly.

But then I felt something give me a push. Immediately I picked my chin up. I waited until I had stopped moving. I looked back, and there you were. I said your name leaping from my seat and into your open arms.

I was crying with joy. We hugged. I never wanted to let you go again. If only that moment would have lasted forever, just like our love.

Chapter 16

The Crash

I hear a screeching sound then a boom and shatter. "BAM!" I heard her scream my name. NO!

I saw it all happen. Those five seconds felt like forever and yet not long enough for me to get to her.

The old, dark blue, pickup truck hit the black ice and blew a flat tire. It was spinning towards her unknown figure.

My Ivory, my best friend, just walking into school. Today was going to be the day I told her. Now she's hurt. I must get to her.

Running as fast as I could push people out of the way in my haste. I had to get to my Ivory. This couldn't be happening. Not her! Please oh please God let her be okay! I thought as I ran.

"Ivory! Ivory! Are you okay? Ivory? Talk to me" I begged when I got to her. She must live. She just must.

Those next five minutes felt like a lifetime. Her emerald eyes shut. They must open again. Her curly strawberry blond hair was spread out and a mess of blood. This can't be happening. She wasn't responding.

Finally, after a lifetime of hurt and pain she groaned. Thank you, God! Thank you!

"Saul? Saul…. Is that you?" she groaned out. It was hard for her to talk I could see that.

"Yes, yes Ivory it's me." My eyes filled with tears. Thank you, God! I thought again. I laid down half on top of her, hugging her, crying. She was okay, my Ivory was okay. "Ivory?" I said between crying.

"Hum?" she groaned out.

"You don't have to say anything, but I just wanted to tell you something...." I hesitated there.

I wasn't sure if I could say it. No, I had to say it. It was Ivory, she was hurt, and I had to. I had waited too long to say it.

Two years I've waited and now I'm going to say it. "Ivory I...I -I love you." I stared crying again, burying my face in her shoulder. "I've loved you for a long time."

"Saul, I love you too. Two years I have." At that point I realized she was hugging me back. It was a weak hug, but I didn't care.

"Sir? Are you hurt?" the ambulances have arrived.

"No, but Ivory is. We need to get her help." I said sitting up and helping the man get to Ivory.

"Arc you, her boyfriend?" the same man said when we got her in the back of the ambulance.

"Yes" Ivory whispered before I could get a word out.

"Come on you can ride in the back with her." I smiled. I was happy and sad. Happy because I finally told my Ivory how I felt. My Ivory was hurt, and I couldn't help her.

The rest of my day was spent in the waiting room with her widowed mother. After an hour of talking to her, I started reading and doing undone math homework.

Ivory would be proud of me since I usually never touch my math homework. An hour of that and I was done.

Finally, what seemed like 10 hours, which was only 5 hours, the nurse finally came out allowing us to see her.

"Ivory?" I said as I walked into her room.

"Saul!" she beamed when she saw me. "I was wondering if you had waited" she was very awake for a car accident victim.

She must be high on pain medications. Sugar always made her sleepy, and I guess the thing that made her awake would make others sleep. Well at least she won't fall asleep when we are talking.

"Hey!" I smiled, I was glad to see her awake, smiling and okay. "Question I have for you."

"Shoot" she was used to me messing up sentences but still making them make sense.

"Can you clarify what's going on between us? Please."

"Simple." She said, grabbing the hand I had on her bed. "Come here I can't move." I leaned in closer to her.

She rolled her eyes and yanked me down to her. Using her not as bruised arm- so our faces were inches apart. "Your best friend status has changed from best to boyfriend."

Then she kissed me! Okay it was a peck on the cheek, but she still kissed me.

I leaned back and sat down in shock. I was still holding her hand, with no intention of letting go.

When the shock wore off, I realized I was smiling, and I couldn't stop. I looked back at her, and she smiled full heartedly at me.

"I guess this means something completely different now?" she said as she held the necklace I gave to her three days ago on her birthday, December 10th. It was a small, silver, raindrop with a cubic zirconium chip.

"No, it doesn't." I shook my head "I gave it to you to show I loved you because I have for the last year. If I gave it to you today, I would give it to you to show my love. It means the same" I smiled, and she smiled back.

"Did I miss something? I was talking to the nurse. Are you two an item?" We both turned to look. Her mom was standing there in the doorway.

I had completely forgotten about her. I went to yank my hand away in embarrassment, but Ivory wouldn't let me.

"I guess that would be a yes for both. Ivory, did they give you morphine? I'll have to talk to them. They should know you get hyper off it. I'll do that later first fill me in on what I missed."

I went to leave to give them some privacy, but Ivory wouldn't let go of my hand.

"Stay!" It wasn't a question it was a demand. I sat back down, and she smiled. She then turned to her mother and filled her in on everything.

I half listened well examining the damage. My left leg broken, bruises everywhere, and stitches on her right cheek a lot better than I thought it would look like. Well at least she's alive.

Two months later

Ivory and I walked down the hall. Her on crunches with a broken left leg and I was holding her books.

We got teased for weeks after the accident, but I didn't care. I had my Ivory, and she was okay. Thank you, God! I thought again for the thousands time since then. Thank you!

"Saul?" she asked when we sat down for math.

"Yeah?"

"Can I ask you something?" She turned her head to face me curiosity filled her eyes.

"You just did but yes you can ask another." I grinned widely.

She rolled her eyes at me and smiled. "Anyway, I was wondering why you were so upset that day."

"Easy, you were hurt, and I was scared that those emerald eyes would never open again. I … I was…" What was I? In love? Yes, in love.

"I was in love, and I hadn't told you …and I wanted to…" my sentence trailed off after that.

"I get it. What happened that day? I don't remember. What I do remember is you. When I opened my eyes I saw blue, but not the blue I wanted.

I was confused and when I saw your face, I saw the blue. The blue I desperately wanted to see.

The color of your eyes then that was it that's all I saw. Your face nothing else I felt you hugging me and heard what you said but that was it that's the first thing I remember then I remember getting out of the car that was it…" she trailed off.

"What happened was…" I don't know if I can tell her. The picture of her broken body, her blood-stained hair, her emerald eyes closed flashed in my mind.

"Cory's truck was going fast.…he hit the black ice.…blew a tire… spinning out of control.…you…just walking.…"

The whole thing past through my mind again. I shuddered at the memory.

She was silent for a minute then she said. "Thank you. I'll never forget. Even if you didn't save me, you were still there for me. Thank you."

I smiled wryly. I still had the horrible picture in my mind.

Two years later

"Saul?" Ivory said, "Come on spit it out Saul." She pushed my dirty blond hair out of my eyes.

I didn't know if I could, I was scared the day I told her I loved her, but that was different.

I thought I had lost her. Now I'm just scared of rejection. Just stupid rejection that was all I feared.

I had to tell her, no ask her. The scene of that day two years ago our senior year of high school passed through my mind again. That day was what helped me finally spit it out.

"Ivory you've been my…best friend for years. I-I just want you to answer a question for me."

I said stumbling over my words. Then, with shaken hands I reached for her left hand and my right pocket.

Pulling out the box and flipping open the box one handed I asked or tried to ask "W-will you marry…" I gulped "Ivory will you marry me" I closed my eyes got on one knee and waited for the answer. You haven't let me down yet God.

Please let her say yes. Please! Those next five minutes of waiting for her to answer felt like déjÃ vu. Me waiting and praying she would answer. Once again it felt like a lifetime.

"Saul?"

"Yes?" I whispered.

"Open your eyes." I did. She leaned down and kissed me. "Yes" she said and kissed me deeper. "Yes! I will!"

I closed my eyes again hugging her tight not wanting to ever let go of her, ever. Thank you, God. Thank you for her, for giving her to me.

The phrase I heard my mom say to my dad in their wedding vows from the video I saw popped into my head at that moment, and I knew it applied to us.

Meeting you was fate, becoming your friend was choice, but falling in love, I had no control over.

Chapter 17

Made for Each Other

Roberto and I have been best friends pretty much since we were born. We grew up living a 5-minute walk away from each other. Our dads were good friends.

We'd always stay at each other's houses, even on school nights. Our parents thought we were basically made for each other and that our future would include the two of us, with children.

They liked the fact that we had each other to lean on and to take care of one another.

I remember the first time when we were little that we thought it'd be cool if we kissed each other, we were probably in second or third grade.

Once we tried it, we thought we'd never want to do it again! Roberto liked to play tricks on me, and he'd always tickle me.

He'd sit on me and try to make me pee my pants. When we were kids, we'd always find some way to goof around and be weird.

Once we got a little older, our parents realized that our hormones would become a little crazier, so we weren't allowed to spend the night together anymore.

We hung out every day, all day until one of our parents called us home. If Roberto wasn't eating dinner at my house, I was eating dinner at his house, or we were eating out together that night.

When we got into middle school everyone knew that we were best friends. Some people tried to spread a rumor saying we've been dating forever or that we just liked to have fun together.

Those people never realized what Roberto and I really had. It was hard dealing with all the things our peers would say about us.

We both knew that we always had each other no matter what. We'd gotten this far in our lives together, what could pull us apart now?

Once we got into high school people immediately told us that we should date. They kept pushing us and pushing us, telling us we'd be the perfect happy couple.

We talked about it a countless number of times, but we both agreed that we had something way too special to start something different.

We were both too comfortable with the way things were that we didn't want to take the risk of completely ruining it.

He was the one guy I knew I could trust with things I wouldn't even tell my parents. I knew he would take my secrets to the grave with him.

Our freshman year went by quickly. Then our sophomore year went by even quicker. Then there was the big junior year, the year of Varsity sports and Prom. He was on the football team in the fall and I played basketball in the winter. I'd go every Friday night to cheer him on and when I looked in the stands to see if he was at my basketball games, he was always sitting front and center.

He always made sure that I knew he was there to support me, and he always knew I was there to support him.

That's how we were, we were practically one person. It was our senior year, on a Thursday; we went out to dinner to a little family diner down the road.

We were just enjoying ourselves as usual, but I could tell something was on Roberto's mind that he wanted to talk about eventually, but he knew now wasn't the time because we were having fun and being our normal selves.

So finally, I built up the courage to ask him what was going on.

"Roberto, what's wrong?" I asked him.

"I don't know that I really want to talk about it. We'll have to eventually but is now really the moment?" he uneasily replied.

"Well, if we're going to have to talk about it eventually, we might as well talk about it now while we still have the time."

There was a slight pause before he decided to speak. "What are we going to do next year when we're in college and going to different schools.

Well, where do you even want to go to college?" A frown came upon his face as he asked me this.

The second I heard his question I knew exactly why he didn't want to talk about it. We had been avoiding the discussion of not going to school together in the years ahead.

We would try to figure out a way to go to the same school, but our majors are just so different it seems almost impossible.

I look up from my food and grab his hand as I can feel the tears beginning to work their way to my eyes.

"We've been best friends all our lives, right? We've been there for each other through all the toughest things we've faced.

You were even there when I was born!" A grin finds its way across my face. "If we've made it this far in our lives and nothing has changed, then I doubt going to different schools will break us apart.

We obviously won't see each other as much, but we'll make things work." As I tell him this, I try to convince myself while the words I am speaking to him are true.

"You never answered my question of where you want to go." He replied a little on the edgy side.

I knew he was upset about the whole situation, but he didn't have to start getting upset with me. "I don't really know yet. I want to study abroad, like in France.

I don't think my parents could afford it right now and I know I certainly couldn't. I'm not sure that any school around here even offers that type of thing.

So, I might have to go out of state. Plus, it'll be nice to get out of Connecticut for a change."

Through the corner of my eye, I could see his posture just slouch once I said that. "I knew we'd be apart, but I didn't think it'd be that far." He couldn't find the words he wanted to say next.

The first thought to float through my head was, what if he came with me. If we weren't dating, then why would I ask him to do something like that.

Friends don't need to see each other every day to keep their relationship strong and going. That was the first time that I had ever even considered being with him in the way that everyone told us we were destined to be.

It made my stomach a little queasy. I didn't know what to do. Roberto could tell something was going on in my head now.

He gave me a puzzled look. Then I had to look away. What was I supposed to do? Tell him that I just figured out that I might want to be with him.

Should I tell him that we've been best friends for our entire lives, and we've had way more than one opportunity to be together, but it took me until the last year before we'll separate to figure out that we might be right together?

What if it's just the thought of leaving him that makes me scared and makes me want anything that can keep us together?

What if I don't really want to be with him like that, I just want to make sure that I don't lose him as a friend?

I can't tell him that I have feelings for him if I don't even know what I'm feeling. Before I could even stop them, the words came out of my mouth. "What if you went with me?"

Maybe to him it wasn't as big of a deal, he didn't see right away how much it would be affecting his life and how he would be giving up so much to be with his best friend, not his girlfriend, fiancé, or wife.

A smile came upon his face, it gave me butterflies. "I wouldn't mind that. Like you said it'd be nice to get out of Connecticut for once."

He used my words to now prove his point. He didn't find this such a big deal, so why did I?

"Would you really leave everything here to go to school with me even though we aren't..."

I couldn't find the right word I wanted to say. ".Together." I finally spat out.

"Is there a chance of us eventually ending up together?"

He was just as surprised as I was that this came up in very serious conversation.

I sat there for a moment still on the edge of tears completely lost and confused as to what I really wanted.

There were butterflies in my stomach like I had never felt before. Maybe this is what I've been waiting for in life to make me even happier.

How could I not see myself, yet everyone else could, that maybe we would be good together. "I... I would be willing to give it a try."

My hand flew over my mouth after I said that. My life just took a drastic turn. I made myself pause for a minute. I closed my eyes, took a deep breath, and that's when I realized.

The butterflies in my stomach grew even bigger than I thought they ever could. I didn't want to show him how vulnerable I was about this situation and for once in my life I couldn't tell what he was feeling or thinking. I never thought we would be in this type of situation.

"Well," he said. "What should we do?"

"Is dating me something you'd actually be interested in?" I was nervous to hear his response.

"Lourdes, I've realized recently that I have wanted to start a relationship with you, but I didn't know how to tell you.

Every time I wanted to tell you I'd look at you and remember everything we have and completely be at a loss for words."

He began to speak a little softer. "I'm just as lost and confused about this as you are. I want to be with you wherever you go.

I want to be there to support you in the hard times that you might face and be there to talk about the tough decisions that you might have to make.

I want to be there to show you that someone loves and cares for you no matter what mistake you make.

Everything is there for us to be together, so why aren't we? Just because we're scared about what's going to happen.

If things don't work out in a more serious situation, we'll figure out a way to get back to normal. If there's a will there's a way.

We can't just leave this the way it's always been. Then wonder for the rest of our lives what it might've been like.

We can't be afraid of what could happen because we'll never know until we try, and I don't want to regret not taking the opportunity to be with you."

He sighed very deeply; I could tell he just got the load of the world off of his chest. He looked up at me and a grin slid across his face. I couldn't help but smile myself.

"How long have you wanted to say all of this to me?" I asked in a concerned manner.

"Once I knew for sure I felt it, I knew I really wanted it.

For a long time, I was just too scared to see it. I kept denying the fact that I thought I wouldn't be able to live without you." He sighed again.

"You never know until you try right?" I kind of smirked as I said this....

The next day we went on our first official date. It wasn't weird, it seemed like it should've been like this all along.

We were both more than happy to know that this might work out for our good. I kept thinking how glad I was that we talked about it and finally figured out what we wanted. It was more than I could've ever expected!

Eventually we just knew we were meant to be. There was no other way we could see our lives.

We discussed it and we decided that it might be a good thing that we didn't start dating in middle school or high school. That situation could've caused us to break up and not be together now.

We knew that we had been best friends for such a long time for a reason. It gave us the opportunity to figure out who we were separately before we had to decide who we were as one.

Our freshman year of college was a lot of fun. We both ended up going to the University of Maryland.

We enjoyed exploring the new atmosphere together. Then there was the one day of my life I know I will never forget.

I was in my room at school just studying for the English test I had the next day. Roberto said he was going to go pick something up. He'd be back in a little bit.

First, he was gone for an hour, and then it turned into three, then four. I kept trying to call his cell phone but there was no answer.

I knew he doesn't like to answer his phone while he's driving but usually if I call him more than once he answers and just quickly talks to me.

Since he wasn't picking up, I called one of his buddies, Al, to see if he knew what was going on and why he was gone for so long.

He said he was going to surprise me with something, but he didn't think it would take that long for him to get it.

I sat there worried, and I kept trying to call but I got nothing. Eventually when I called him it went right to his voicemail, I couldn't help but assume the worst.

At around 2 o'clock in the morning Roberto's dad called me. He told me that the State of Maryland police had called him and told him that Roberto was in a very serious car accident.

He didn't know what was going to happen to him. He was conscious but he had no idea what was going on. The police were sending him straight to the hospital to get checked out.

Once I got all the hospital information I went straight to my car and drove to the hospital.

I never thought it was so far away, it seemed like it took me forever to get there that night. It felt like I couldn't breathe, my chest felt like it had a thousand pounds on it the entire way there.

The walk down the hall to what might have been my biggest nightmare was the most devastating.

I've cried before but I have never cried that hard. Thoughts just kept going through my head that he might not be there for me tomorrow morning.

I couldn't get over the fact that I've lived my entire life with this man and that I might not have him anymore.

I finally reached his room. I tried to wipe my tears away and act like everything was ok because I didn't want to scare him. I wanted to show him that in his vulnerable situation I would be strong for him.

I took a deep breath before I walked in because I knew this would be something I could never prepare myself for.

I walked in, turned the corner and there he was. His eyes were shut, and I could hardly tell his chest was moving up and down.

He had cuts and scrapes all over. There were bright orange casts on his left arm and leg. I was at a loss of breath when first saw him.

I grabbed his hand, and he opened his eyes just slightly. A grin crawled across his face when he saw that it was me.

I couldn't help myself; I started bawling. I carefully sat next to him on the bed and hugged him.

He told me that everything was going to be ok and that he was going to make it through this.

He reassured me that he'd be there for me for the rest of my life no matter what. He told me that he loved me and that he'd fight through anything to stay with me.

I sat up and he wiped my tears with his unbroken arm. I apologized for the way I was acting.

He tried to explain what happened, but he said it all happened so fast that he didn't really know what occurred.

When he stopped talking, I looked to the right of his bed and on the nightstand was a little black box.

When I saw it, I gasped. I wasn't positive that I knew what it was but I kind of figured. He tried to turn it over and grabbed it.

He held it in his hand for a minute just staring at it as tears started to stream down his cheeks.

He looked up at me, his eyes full of tears and told me that this wasn't the way he wanted to do this.

He wanted to make it perfect for me, a moment he knew I could never forget. He opened it and the second I saw the gorgeous diamond ring sitting in the velvet slit of the box I felt the tears begin to run down my cheeks again.

He didn't even have to say anything before I said yes. He put the ring on my finger and hugged me more passionately than ever before.

I had never felt such different feelings at the same time. I was sad and confused about what was going on with him and his physical health. But at the same time, I was so happy I didn't know what to do with myself.

Roberto came home with me safely a couple days after he entered the hospital. The doctors wanted to make sure that everything was alright and would go back to normal.

There were a few tough months of rehab and getting Roberto better. But once we knew he was ok to travel again, we both took some time off from school and go back home to visit our parents.

It was good to be in the comfort of our homes and be in the places that we grew up together and made all those awesome memories.

While we were sitting there with our families, we started discussing the date of our wedding and some of the things we thought we might be interested in having.

That was the first day that it really hit me that our families after all this time would finally become one.

If someone would've told us that we were going to be getting married someday, we would tell them that they were completely crazy, and they had no idea what they were talking about.

But there we were, in a situation that I never thought we'd be in. But at that time in our lives, I wasn't complaining.

The wedding plans took a long time. We finally decided that we wanted to get married in the spring, April 22nd to be exact.

We took our time figuring out exactly what we wanted to make it the wedding of our dreams.

Today's the day. There are so many things running through my mind, but I'm not stressed at all.

I keep reminding myself that I've known this man for my entire life and how we've been through literally everything together.

So even if something did go wrong on this wonderful day, if he's there and I'm there, everything will be fine.

The only thing I can't get myself to calm down is my nerves. He's always told me that I'm beautiful, but there's nothing like being in a wedding dress.

People expect you to look the most gorgeous you ever have in your entire life; I just want to know if he thinks that.

One thing I've really looked forward to is walking down the aisle and seeing my fiancé's face when he first sees me.

It's moments before I am supposed to walk down the aisle, I'm starting to get choked up remembering all these things that we've been through. I look to my dad for comfort, he's no better because he's choked up too. But even though he is upset he reminds me that he would rather give me to Roberto than any other man on the earth.

I don't want to cry as I go down the aisle; I want to have the brightest of smiles. Memories of funny times with Roberto are beginning to pop into my head.

Some of them are even making me laugh a little. Music is playing again, the very familiar tune.

It brings me back to the reality of it being my own wedding day. I must take a deep breath before my dad, and I start walking.

There he was at the front of the church. We made eye contact, and I could tell there were tears gathering in his eyes.

I'm doing everything I can to keep myself smiling and not crying. I never thought my wedding would be this emotional.

My dad and I got up to the front and he gave me to Roberto. Once I feel the touch of Roberto's hand everything seems so much calmer.

We turn towards the pastor and the service begins. The next thing I know I feel the slight chill of the silver ring sliding onto my finger and I hear him speak the words, "I do."

Tears are running down my cheeks as I remember that one time in my life, I was afraid that I'd never get this opportunity.

Now here it is and it's the happiest moment of my entire life. I look him in the eye, and he gives me a smile of comfort. I take his ring and speak the words, "I do."

Chapter 18

My Guardian Angel

I used to know how to do everything, understand everything. That was before, and now I can't.

People come to me now and give me looks of pity, but words of normality. They think that just because my ears don't work, I'm blind as well and can't see their looks of sympathy.

In the past everyone would just joke around and laugh with me, as people usually do. Everything is different now.

The doctor says that my hearing will get worse until I'll be completely deaf. If not for the doctor's visit I would think the world was just quiet, and I wasn't deaf, at least I wouldn't admit to that fact.

My closest friends and even my family avoid me like a plague. Before I could listen to the beauty of the world, I would ignore it.

The birds would sing, the wind would howl, but I would be caught up with the fast-paced life I led, as was and is the way of the world.

All I have left are memories of that sound. I miss all the things I could do with my voice. Now I can barely speak, and half the time, don't even know what I'm saying.

The next morning, on Saturday, I went out. The brisk, autumn wind gently swirled around me. I took a walk around the park, following the rocky, gravel trail laid before me.

Then the next thing I remember is that he appeared. Him, with his dark, shaggy hair, and golden eyes, with pink lips and pale skin.

He looked at me, and his lips moved calling out to me. I couldn't hear what he said, and signed that "I cannot understand, I'm deaf."

Apparently, he knew sign language too, and walked over and said hello. I don't know what happened, but he entranced me, and we began talking.

The day was filled with some sort of subtle magic. We walked around the path about 7 times, and it was twilight when we said good-bye.

"I'll see you tomorrow," he said.

I don't know how he found me the next morning, but I ran into him at church. The service had just ended, and I found him standing there talking to the pastor.

He spotted me, excused himself, and started to walk toward me. I didn't understand why, but I couldn't move.

My legs weren't disabled, but it felt as though iron weights chained me to the earth.

Suddenly, he was standing right in front of me. He gave me a grateful smile and led me out through the wooden doors of the church.

We spent the whole day together, and the following Monday he was there as well. I found him talking to the receptionist.

This time I went up to him and said hello. I found myself offering to show him around the school.

My heartbeat increased, as fast as a hummingbird, with every step I took. I never noticed anything but him when we were together, it felt so right.

I forgot all about what happened to me. I forgot about my friend's and family's empathy, and all the other troubles I had.

Soon, the day was over. My nerves tired from being over the edge, knowing that he was in my school and that he could be anywhere. But after the tour, I never saw him.

After school, I went over to the football field, and he was there. I guess I shouldn't be surprised, he was almost everywhere I went.

Then I saw it happen. The girl he was talking to just leaned up and kissed him. It was after that betrayal he saw me.

I didn't even stop to think, I just ran away fast and hard. My heart was crushed, almost as if I had been holding up the sky, and now it was crashing down over me. It was treason!

I wasn't even aware I was running to the park where I first met him. I just walked around, like a mindless robot, unfeeling and unthinking.

The next day, I missed school. I didn't see him for the entire day. He found me; he always did. No words were exchanged, only feelings. I was just walking around the park again, and he was there, the same as when I first saw him.

I didn't even feel like running, so I just turned my head and stormed off. I saw him following me then, running up and holding me prisoner in his arms.

The world didn't move, and for a second, I was blind. All I could feel were his arms binding on me, overpowering my weak restraint.

His lips were pressed gently to mine, and he kissed me filling my heart with passion and ecstasy I never knew existed.

It was in that moment that I knew he was mine. Then everything else didn't matter anymore.

I didn't care that I was deaf, that my friends and family avoided me, or that he was kissed by another girl. All that mattered was that he was mine. I surrendered myself to him, and the rest of the world just faded away.

Chapter 19

Just Friend

I watch her as she flirts with other guys. It always breaks my heart. Every now and then she catches me watching.

She gets this confused look on her face. I hope I can use her as much as she uses me.

She waves me over with a smile on her face. I pull on the mask once again and walk over. The once confidante guy shrinks away. It sucks not being able to talk to your best friend.

Chapter 20

I Do

It ended with I do. That's what I think of every time I think of my first date. It was the perfect night, I thought to myself, remembering my first date with my husband Ray.

It was many years ago, but I can still remember every detail with perfect clarity. I was so nervous because it was my first date with John, who I had been in love with for what seemed like an eternity, but it was my first date ever.

I spent a long time getting ready, straightening my hair, painting my nails, and going through a million outfits. At about seven, when he was supposed to pick me up, I was finally ready.

Before bounding down the stairs, I took one last look in the mirror. "Perfect," I thought to myself. When I got downstairs, John had arrived and was talking to my parents in the living room.

Looking at my parents, I could tell immediately that they liked him, but then again, what's not to like? He was a strong Christian, a gentleman who was nice to everyone, had a great sense of humor, and great looking. What more could I ask for?

I had been good friends with John for years, but it was only a couple days before that we found out we both wanted to be more than friends. Seeing him waiting for me left me breathless.

I couldn't believe it; he liked me more than a friend! We left shortly after that. He took me to dinner and then to a movie.

What we did on our date I realize doesn't sound all that exciting, but it was to us, two sixteen-year-olds who were just enjoying talking and being with each other. It was the perfect night; as perfect as anything in this life can be, everything felt completely magical, like nothing could go wrong!

After the movie, he drove to the beach where we walked hand in hand, talking, and taking in the beauty of the scenery.

After that, he took me home. I didn't want it to end, but after that night, we spent time with each other almost every day, at school, church, and in our free time.

Then, on my 25th birthday, fifty years ago today, on a walk in the park, he got down on one knee and proposed. Soon after that we were married, and it has been a miracle ever since.

Even now as I look at him, I feel the same love for him I felt then, and I know it's a love from God. It hasn't all been perfect, nothing ever is, but it's been close. And it all started with that first, perfect date.

Chapter 21

There are no Words

"Do you think I am easier to be played on than a pipe?" I ask. I couldn't hold myself back anymore. She was looking at me with her eyes open wide, her mouth open; she was at a loss of words for once.

"I can't believe you!"

"I'm sorry" she says.

"What about last night? Did that mean nothing to you?" I take a couple steps back from her "You told me that you lo…"

"It didn't mean anything."

"You said you didn't care about him that you really wanted to be with me!"

"I said it didn't mean anything" she repeats, like an underfed parrot.

I sat on the bed, when I found the courage to look at her; I saw her blue eyes looking right back at me.

A single tear rolls down her cheek, I stand up again and try to wipe away her tear, but she pushes my hand away. I sit back down.

"I was drunk" she says, "It didn't mean anything."

"Weakness, thy name is woman!" She brings her hand up to her face, as if putting a barrier in between us.

"Just because you were drunk doesn't mean there wasn't truth in your words. You told me you loved me, not him."

"Why now?" she says. "Why did you have to tell me now? He says he loves me, and now you're telling me the same, I don't know what to do."

"Do you have any feelings for him?"

"I… I don't know… it's just that…"

"It's a simple question; do you or do you not have feelings for him?"

"Yes," she says.

"God had given you one face and you make yourselves another. You were just telling me last night on how little he meant to you."

"I'm so sorry" She sits down beside me and reaches for my hand and holds it, letting our fingers in twine. I want her more than anything.

"What are you doing with him?" I ask. "He can never love you like I can. He doesn't know you. You need someone who loves you unconditionally, who doesn't care if you are too lazy to put on makeup, who doesn't need you to dress up for him." I pause, taking in a breath. "I'm that guy."

"What about him" she says. "He says that he loves me." "I know him better than you do. You two have nothing in common; your relationship is and never will be anything more than just a physical attraction.

Call it what you want, but you and me both know that it isn't love." I stare at her, choking back tears I just stare at her.

We are so close I can see my reflection in her eyes. I move my head forward to kiss her, but I stop myself.

"I can't do it" I say. "You say you love me one day and have feelings for someone else the next. You can't treat me like this; I need an answer from you. Will it be my heart, or will it by his?"

She opens her mouth as if to speak, but no words come out. She tears her gaze away, not able to look at me.

"Perfect" I say, "just perfect." I grab my coat and head for the door. I look back at her, hoping she will say something, but she still can't bring herself to look at me. I put on my coat and walk out the door.

Chapter 22

The Many Memories

He looked to the black Mercedes. She was gone. All he could do was to look, to watch, for any sign.

It started raining again, but he did not notice. She was gone. What else could he do now? No more walking around the flower shop and smelling the sweetness of the spring flowers.

No more going into the kitchen of his father's candy shop to steal the candies he has just baked. No more the tree.

Oh, the tree.

It seems like they've spent the entire summer under that tree. They just walked to the park and sit. They used to sit under that same tree day after day, used to eat the candies he'd just stolen and talk until the sun decided to hide itself beyond the mountains.

They always wanted more time. He wanted to admire those green eyes and she wanted to look at his silly smile. Just a little more, he thought. Just a little. But the moon was already crossing the sky and the stars already started to appear in the dark-blue sky. It was time to go.

Then he guided her across the streets, where earlier children played soccer. He took her home, gave her a goodnight kiss and walked home.

As he crossed the empty streets, he was already thinking about spending the day with her tomorrow.

But no more because now the black Mercedes was crossing the same streets where he'd guided her.

He could see on the window of the black Mercedes the girl looking at him. He could see as the green eyes, he'd admired so much, watered. He wanted to kiss her once again and hug her and say goodbye.

But no more. The black Mercedes turned the corner in the end of the street and disappeared into the rain and the night.

All he wanted was a little more time with her. The sun already hidden between the mountains and now the stars did not appear. They wouldn't, because now a storm was approaching. He wanted to see the sun, the moon, the tree, and those green eyes again.

It was cold, raining and she was gone. His father guided him across the pavement into his house.

'Come on', he said as he guided his son back home. 'You have school tomorrow.'.

Chapter 23

The Magic Hands

The quiet rustling of the leaves and trickling droplets of water spun together a calming melody that danced with the swirling breeze.

The burning heat was reduced by waves of sea foam magic. Once the first color starts to hit the canvas, the picture slowly starts to trickle into a lifeless grey wash.

A girl stood in front of the canvas, the woven fabric, now in the delusional mind of light fluffy clouds.

Her strokes started to create shapes, shapes began to create objects and the yin-yang shades began to create a black-white perspective.

Strokes, shapes, and shades is all what different ideas needed to create an imaginative landscape, where hills elapsed into white elephants and where coffee-colored grosbeaks breaded their babies in white fields of daisies.

An acid fragrance overwhelmed the sea breeze as she tenderly twisted off the caps of fresh gouache paint.

Sitting by the seashore, she squinted her ocean blue eyes, tilting her prim oriental face so that strands of strawberry blonde hair slipped onto her face.

She stretched her porcelain hands, as the sleeves of her cotton dress bled into the pink designs of peony blossoms. Using her extended fingers, she picked up the brush,

She began to confidently wash away her introduction of grey, replacing it with shades of pacific, cerulean, sapphire and periwinkle blue to create a doppelgänger, of the very same sea foam sorcery beholding her naked eyes.

Forming ripples in her dilation of the sea, her pearl shades of white represent Lord Vishnu's conch shell as it illuminated the nightly atmosphere of the canvas with scattered stars and constellations.

Yet again, stroke by stroke came to life, with fluttering remains of a golden veil and a young girl wedging her asymmetrical toes in the sand as denim waves wash her feet.

It wasn't perfect like her mam's sweet apple pie or granny's yellow rose garden.

Yet the girl smiled as the sun kissed moon, as the starry night sky dazzled upon her, realizing it's just the pelicans and the sea's soul breathing in and out.

She lay down on the sand, as the night sky exhaled. Whispering the remaining words of her painting to the sand, "never have I ever...

Chapter 24

Husband and Wife

An empty aisle of no return Showered in ruffles and bows One step goes after another, Am I making a mistake?

The eyes from one person shine out from all the rest

I realized it in the past And I realize it now,

Our past is shining out into my future Memories if single tears shine out the most

I spent years thinking about your face, I spent days dreaming of your smile

And every time you hurt and pushed me away, I became closer to our truth.

So, now here I stand, next to you. This is no mistake, for us forever will never end

But our lives as two people does end. We are now one, together for as long as we both shall live, we are now and forever will be Husband and Wife...

Chapter 25

The Bridge

Freddy saw before him the bridge. It was a dark, flaky brown, signifying centuries of rust. It groaned continuously, a menacing groan yet strangely welcoming.

He stared at the steel support beams that loomed several yards above him. Lowering his gaze to eye level, he saw the engulfing blackness across the bridge.

Breezes pulsed in and out like a breathing creature, and he saw the movement of the night. A hand stretched forth, a chalky white hand that seemed to have been worn over the years.

With its palm upwards, it moved but a single finger to usher him forward. Without the will to resist he followed and saw just above the hand a pair of crimson eyes staring at him.

Everything seemed distorted as he struggled against himself, trying to pull away. The darkness faded as he approached the owner of the red eyes and ashen hand. He could not look at first, then began to raise his head.

Freddy Quinones shot up on his bed with a gasp. His heavy breathing was shaky and drenched in sweat. The small wooden room seemed to close in around him. A whistle from a breeze through the window carried a strange horror.

He looked down at his pregnant wife, Alma, who was lying peacefully next to him. Her steady breathing comforted him, and he lowered himself again.

Dark shadows lined the uneven ceiling as he looked up, and he thought he could see the crimson eyes staring at him.

The next morning, he awoke to the pale morning sun. Cold breezes flooded into the room, battling with the blazing heat of the fireplace on the wall opposite Feart. Winter was coming fast. He would have to harvest the remaining crops out in the field before the first snow.

He looked over to find that his wife was already up and in the kitchen. Feart still felt shaken from the dream he had had that night, but the light of the sun scattered his fears away.

Dressing quickly, Freddy walked out into the short hallway connecting all the rooms upstairs. Several quick bounds put him in front of a tall wooden door, much the same as the rest of the doors in the house.

With a painful creak of the hinges, he peered inside the room. There lying in the bed on the opposite wall was his daughter, Lily. Her eyes were staring at the door in anticipation.

When she saw Freddy, her eyes lit up, crying "Daddy!" She hopped out of bed and rushed over to him in her small nightgown, wrapping her small arms around Feart's kneecaps.

"Daddy's here!" he said, trying to mimic Lily's tone. He scooped her up to his shoulder and looked her in the eye. "I've got to go now, Lily. I'm going to be out in the fields."

The gleam in Lily's eyes faded somewhat, "When will you be back?"

Feart, not wanting to disappoint her further, struggled furiously to find a way to see her at lunch. "I'll be back before lunch, okay?"

"Okay…" she responded.

Freddy laid her back in the small bed and promptly left the room. When he arrived downstairs, he found Alma making eggs over the fireplace.

"Won't you have some breakfast?" Alma looked at him and gestured with the pan holding the eggs. Her eyes flowed with genuine concern. She knew what Feart had endured.

Almost half of the vegetables and a good portion of the livestock had either died of disease, malnutrition or from the freezing cold.

There was hardly enough to sustain the family through the entire winter, and with a new baby coming, it would get even harder.

Freddy walked forward and kissed Alma, holding the embrace for a moment until she pulled away. Feart then saw a gleam of remorse and sorrow, but she blinked, and it was gone.

"I've promised our daughter that I would be back by lunch, and I'll need all the time I can get to harvest the remaining crops." Freddy laid a hand on Alma's stomach, "Take care of our children. Both."

Then he turned and left through the front door, throwing on a light coat, and grabbing his shovel and hoe.

"Take care," Alma whispered behind him. Freddy walked quickly out into the lengthy field behind the small house. No tree rose from the ground for miles, giving Freddy the time, he needed to think.

He walked along a winding path, his mind wandering past the trees and the mountains that encircled the tiny village in its tiny valley. He soon arrived at the bridge, which stretched across a ravine at the other end of the valley.

His dream returned to him once again, and he saw those piercing eyes. In his mind he walked past them and into the darkness beyond.

No one who went across the bridge ever came back, but somehow the stories did. Stories of great buildings, towering hundreds of feet above you, of machines that rolled along, even uphill, with no horses to pull them.

There were even stories of flying machines, with huge wings that spanned a hundred feet, and they glided through the air like a bird.

Freddy could never bring himself to believe in these stories, even though a large portion of him wanted more than anything to believe in such magical things.

He awoke from his daydream to find that he had stumbled upon his last remaining turnip crop.

He set to work immediately, using both of his tools to uproot the plants. The cold air had solidified the soil, making his job very difficult.

As he dug up the first turnip, Freddy immediately saw that it had frozen. Now it was inedible. He threw down the plant in frustration and released a terrible bellow.

The sound echoed through the field, like hundreds of farmers crying out in aggravation. He began again on the opposite side of the crop, but to no avail.

All the turnips had frozen over, signifying a years' worth of time wasted. Only about two of the plants survived, and these he cared for by the stems. With his attitude boiling, he made his way through the cold of early November.

When he had arrived back at the house, Lily was sitting on the steps picking at a daisy. Strange, that a daisy would still be so vibrant even this late in autumn.

She stroked the pedals lovingly, as if they were alive. The innocence in her gaze poked at his conscience. What will he do in the dead of winter when she must go to bed hungry because he couldn't feed her?

Freddy walked over to her and laid a hand on her shoulder. She looked up at him with her round green eyes.

"Daddy," she said and jumped up to hug him around the leg. It took him a moment to respond, for he was lost in his own thoughts of the fast-approaching winter.

"Daddy's back," he whispered quietly as he propped her up on his shoulder.

With Lily leaning against his head, Freddy made his way through the front door and into the narrow kitchen.

There was barely enough room to fit a table, so usually Alma cooked outside by a large fire for important meals like lunch and supper. She was sitting there at the table with the meal already laid out, a slight smile on her face and her arms lay out across the table.

Freddy sat head-to-head to Alma and placed Lily down in the seat across from him. They ate in silence, as was custom, and only began to talk after everyone was finished.

"So," began Alma, "How are the fields?"

"Good, good. Everything is going well." From the look in Alma's face, he could see that she did not believe him.

Lily looked at both parents with intense eyes, trying to see the reason for Freddy and Alma's tension, but to no benefit.

"Today I found a meadow of flowers," she began cautiously, "There were pretty blue flowers, but the white ones were my favorites."

Freddy looked up at Alma and then to Lily, "That's great Lily. Where was the meadow?"

Lily's eyes brightened at this comment, excited that her father was interested, "It was in the forest, next to a long path and a big brown bridge!"

Her eyes were large as she ate some soup. Freddy felt the dream rush back to him again, seeing the old, rusted bridge before him, moaning, and the dark figure standing before him.

Then his mind wandered off beyond the dark behind the figure, and the great things that were supposed to be there. "Daddy?" Lily's voice pierced his thoughts, "Daddy, are you okay?"

Freddy blinked his eyes to find that he was still in the kitchen with Alma and Lily. Alma was looking at him concernedly. Lily was looking at him with curiosity. "Are you okay Freddy?" Alma came over to him and laid a hand over his forehead.

"No, you don't seem to have a fever. You were staring off into space for almost ten minutes."

"I'm fine," he responded. The small kitchen seemed a little darker now. Freddy rose from his chair and kissed Alma softly. "Ten minutes? If that's the case,

I must be off now." Freddy went over and hugged Lily. She still seemed curious and didn't complain at his leave as she normally would.

"Okay," Lily looked at Freddy.

"Ten minutes? Is that all you take to eat lunch?" Alma grasped Freddy on the shoulders and laid her chin on his shoulder. "Don't take too long at the bar."

Freddy smiled. "You don't need to worry. I won't." Alma rolled her eyes.

"How many times have I heard that?"

Freddy walked through the main street, taking in the sweet smell of the bakery. Smoke filled the chimneys and the smith's furnace, warming the air around the area.

The noise and the light stream of people moving around was enough to draw Freddy's attention away from his thoughts. He wanted more than anything to be free of them.

He entered the bar, and as soon as he did, he was blasted by the warm air of the fireplace.

Gerry, one of the town elders, was in the middle of one of his famous stories, of the times before the famine, and of great things that went on in the valley before most of the clients in the bar were born.

"… and I struck it down with all my might, only to find that it had fled into the forest in that moment of hesitation.

To this day, it may yet inhabit the woods around the valley." A moment of silence, then great applause.

Freddy joined in, even though he had no idea what the story was about. With a beer in hand, Gerry began another tale.

"This one is called the great war between the vegetarians and the carnivores.'" Freddy had heard this one before, about how the village had split in two.

One side was the vegetarians, who only wanted to eat plants, and the other was the carnivores, who only ate meat.

The war began when the vegetarians stole all the animals from the carnivores, trying to save them, and the carnivores attacked the vegetarians with torches and spears.

Freddy listened until Gerry was finished, when the vegetarians and the carnivores had finally agreed to stop fighting each other, and finally everyone moved back with each other.

"Ah, Freddy, it's good to see you. I was just recounting that ale to the younglings who hadn't heard it yet."

Gerry took a seat next to Freddy. He had a somber look on his face, as if he had something heavy on his mind. "What's wrong?" he thought, and his mouth worked simultaneously. Gerry seemed startled by the question.

"I'm just worried about the village."

Freddy pursued further. "What's wrong?" he repeated.

"The villagers, Freddy, the villagers. They're all going over that rusted bridge. If anyone else goes over the bridge, our village will collapse.

The smiths and craftsman will starve and in turn the farmers will wear out the tools they are using to farm and starve themselves."

Gerry placed his head in his hands. "So many people are leaving. Just this month almost twenty went over the bridge, looking for a greater living, trying to escape the temporary famine."

He put extra emphasis on the temporary. Freddy didn't know what to say, so he remained quiet.

How could he have been so unobservant? Twenty people in a month and he thought that the village was just fine.

He might have even gone over the bridge himself because of the lack of food.

"I'm putting a night guard on duty, to try to stop people from leaving.

We simply can't afford it, we simply can't..." Gerry began to weep and left the bar.

Freddy sat there until nightfall, listening to the stories that the other elders told, his mind never wandering from what Gerry had said.

"Freddy." Alma sat up in bed. She was fully dressed in thick winter clothing. "Could I talk to you?"

"Certainly, Alma, what would you want to talk about?"

Alma rose from the bed, "I want to take a walk."

They walked outside, arm in arm, but Freddy felt dread build up in him. The hairs on his neck stood on end.

Why would Alma want to talk to him during the night, walking in the blistering cold.

They soon reached the bridge and Alma looked over longingly at it. Freddy immediately saw what she intended to do, and he pulled away with all his might.

"No, Alma, you wouldn't." Alma gripped his arm tightly, holding him against all his strength. He did not want to fight her, in fact, that was the last thing he wanted to do. He stopped struggling.

It was like a dream. Alma released him and walked onto the bridge. Freddy followed her silently.

Alma's pale skin shone in the moonlight, and her eyes appeared crimson in the dark. "Please, Freddy, come with me."

She had one hand on his forearm, and the other was placed across her pregnant belly.

He had an obligation to that baby, and if he were not there when he was born, it would be an irreversible blow to his pride.

Her loved Alma, more than anyone. Freddy's gaze drifted back to the village. It looked so peaceful nestled on a hillside in a small valley nestled between the mountains.

The snow covering the rooftops and the smoke flowing from the chimneys never looked so appealing.

He pictured Lily in her bed, sound asleep. He loved Lily as well. The bridge moaned under their combined weight.

Shouts and cries came from the path below. One of the night guards must have spotted both.

It would have looked very suspicious, a couple walking up the path to the bridge in the middle of the night.

The villagers would never allow another farmer to slip out of their midst. Freddy would not be able to go to Lily and bring her back with them.

"Please, Freddy, please. We don't have much time." He looked again at Alma. She signaled him to go with her, tears streaming down her cheeks.

He looked back at the village on the hillside. "We don't have to go far. Once we make it out of the woods, the people on the other side will be able to tend to our every need."

Yes, Freddy would like that. The sound of the villagers grew louder. "Please!" He again pictured Lily, crying when she found that her father had abandoned her, but wouldn't the baby Alma be carrying do the same?

Freddy bent down and picked up a flower from the ground adjacent to the bridge.

It was a lily.

So, dear reader, which did he choose....

The valley or the bridge?

Chapter 26

Emotions

Everything was perfect. The blue waves gently tapping the shore, the cloudless sky, the booming, distant music carried by the restless breeze through the trees.

Serenity filled my heart-broken body as I gazed into his welcoming eyes. I lay there for a while; we said nothing.

Then again, nothing really needed to be said. Everything was already known. This was foreign to me, a subconscious knowing; a beautiful, unspoken unity.

I could feel it vibrating off the very rock we were sitting on. We were no longer two strangers tossed together, uncertain of what we were searching for or why we were there in that moment sitting together.

Both of us did know that we had found something that no one else could understand.

The throbbing in my heart eased as he wrapped his arms around me. I was finally at peace.

Although I was dizzy from looking through the kaleidoscope of my emotions, his comforting touch soothed me. I inhaled the sweet lake air and sighed, my body relaxing into his.

Chicago's skyline danced in the distance while boats played in the seemingly endless, but conquerable Lake Michigan.

Everything faded while I was with him, like the blurring edges of an old photograph. It was just us together on the rocks.

Nothing else mattered. Not the huge crowds of confused college students surrounding us, not the blaring rock music, not the anxious police, not the girls screaming and laughing in the water next to us, not the neighboring couples on rocks, not the birds circling nearby. Nothing.

The whirlwind of life stopped for those few moments, and in those few moments I realized what life is about. It's about the unexpected when you can escape, and you discover something that you'd never think you'd find.

Maybe it's impossible to describe and fully understand exactly what I felt and found that day on those rocks, but every time I look into his eyes, I return to that moment of serenity and the burdens of life are lifted off my shoulders.

It is a pure and raw connection, a rare harmony I found among the tumults of life. In retrospect, I feel fortunate to have experienced such a moment: Ben and me and the rocks. And I hope to have many more.

Chapter 27

The Promise

"Promise me you'll come back, and we'll meet again," said Harry. "Will you promise to wait for me?" I said.

"Yes", said Harry with his beautiful smile. One day the boy and I made a promise that we would meet again no matter what and sit under the big oak tree in the park and talk till' the sun set.

That was 10 years ago and now I'm 15, a sophomore in high school, but I still haven't forgotten that boy I meet everyday day under the big oak tree with the beautiful smile.

Now I am going to fulfill that promise because I am transferring to Casper High in Casper, Wyoming.

I used to live in Casper when I was little but then my father got a job in Miami, Florida and we moved.

Harry and I took it harder than anyone else when we heard about my family moving.

That's why I promised to come back, and Harry promised to wait for me. I cried the whole day when we moved.

After seven hours of begging, I finally got my mom to let me go to Wyoming alone except for calling every day of course. Add another two days packing and unpacking things and were done.

I was extremely excited for school today. I never thought I would say that because I always thought school was a waste of time and space in my life but today, I might see Harry.

He probably doesn't look the same but there's one thing that separates him from the rest, that beautiful smile.

The one I would die for. I know what you're thinking, I'm crazy but he was perfect. Smart, gorgeous, hardworking, fun to be with, and the biggest problem of all is every time I even think about when I was with him my heart goes crazy, I start to blush.

I even giggled a little. I have what my mother calls a big bit from the love bug. I haven't changed so I hope I'm hoping he hasn't either.

Casper High is a very big school, and everything was so different but still the same. Different clothes and buildings, same kind of people.

You would think the transfer student was nervous like crazy, not me. I was not nervous at all; I didn't come to school for any of them just for him.

I observed everything in the classroom very carefully, looking at the room and everyone in it, when I suddenly felt something hit the back of my neck.

I touched my back, and it was a spit- ball! "Ew, that's gross!" All I heard in the background was a boy with black hair, pulled back showing a gorgeous face that was laughing at me.

"Sorry I must have missed", all the class started laughing at me, and I was so embarrassed! I got up and slapped him. "Ouch that hurt!" the jerk said. "Good I didn't miss.", I said with a satisfied look on my face. I walked away knowing he was lucky; I could have done worse.

After class I was still upset about that jerk, so I decided to go where I always go to relax in my favorite place in the world, the big oak tree.

I was sitting down so relaxed and soothed when I heard crying. When I turned around it was the jerk and a little girl who was crying.

Making little girls cry, somehow, I didn't feel surprised. I was about to walk up to him to tell him to stop picking on little girl and to pick and someone his own size, when I heard "Why are you crying little girl?", "I don't know where my mommy is?" cried the little girl.

"It's okay I will stay and look for mommy with you, okay?", "Okay, thanks mister", smiled the little girl. "Let's go then" and they walked away.

That was weird I thought. Why was the jerk not acting like a jerk? And why was here, at the park and what for? These three things I thought a lot about as I walked home.

In the morning I was excited as usual for school. Thinking maybe he didn't go to school yesterday because he was absent and is coming today.

I raced to school only to be disappointed again, he must be absent again. This was the only high school in Wyoming and the worst part of all was he wasn't there, and the jerk was. Sitting where he always sits, on the left in the corner at the end of the row. But I did learn something today; my enemy's name is Jose Davila.

That name, I knew it somewhere but oh well I am very forgetful. If I wasn't I wouldn't be in this mess.

After school again I decided to sit in my special place under the tree, only to find Jose sitting there.

"Move, that's my spot!" I was so upset thinking he used it there, replaced with that jerk Jose.

He looked up at me and then said, "You don't own this tree. Secondly, I know you're mad at me about the spitball but honestly it was a mistake, I didn't mean to.

Finally, I come here every single day waiting for a friend under this tree. She moved away but I come here every single day to..." he stops and then looked away. "To fulfill the promise, right?"

He looked at me with shock in his eyes. "Leida?" he asked. "Yea", I said with a smile on my face. He grabbed me and we hugged each other. "Please never leave me.", "I would dream of it", I said. He smiled that beautiful, gorgeous smile. At that moment I knew for sure that I had finally found him, my Jose!

Chapter 28

The Stalker

As I was walking down the hall where the sophomore lockers were, I bumped into Nilsa. Everyone knew her and everyone hated her.

She butted into everyone's conversation. Everywhere you where she was there just sitting there staring at you, listening to every bit of the conversation.

Nilsa was known as the 'Stalker' because of her ability to follow you around when you didn't want her to.

If you talked about her and she found out, she would run to her mother and cry about it until her mom called the school. Normally the school did nothing about it. The whole entire county hated the family; they were just too creepy and too obnoxious.

After I said I was sorry she initially started a long and boring conversation which was more like a monologue about her mom letting her finally get a kitten.

I was so bored and wanted to leave but I couldn't because she would cry if I just walked away. It was too early to think of a way to say goodbye nicely.

As I was standing there patiently listening, Ray turned around the corner. He saw the look of desperation mixed with boredom on my face and said," Hey Nilsa, Mr. P. wants to see A.S.A.P."

"Okay I'll get right on it, thanks," I replied. I ran towards my locker and breathed a sigh of relief when Ray caught up with me. "Thanks for saving me that was the worst thing in the world." I told him.

"No problem, when I see a damsel in distress, I immediately break out my shining armor."

"I thank you very much Sir Lancelot... although that line was pretty cheesy."

"So, what are you doing tonight?'" He asked in an innocent voice as if he was clueless.

I played along, "Uh... I don't know... maybe play in my basketball game and then rush to get to the school dance.

"Oh... sounds interesting. So, I was wondering if your dad could drive me to the game and then maybe give me another lift to the dance."

"I don't see why he couldn't. Don't forget that my game is at 6:30 though."

"I won't. So, I will see you at lunch, alright."

"Alright, see you later."

The bell rang and I ran to first block which is Spanish today for me. I got in the classroom just in time and was reluctant to see Lizzie sitting in the back with a seat with my name on it. "Hey," she said with a big smile on her face.

I sat down, then the teacher, Mrs. Chaqueta walked in and sat down. She grabbed a piece of paper, scribbled something, and then took attendance. When she was finished, she said, "You are going to have a project due when you come back from break."

Chapter 29

Loving Someone

Over the summer, I met the most amazing girl named Norma at the beach. She had beautiful flowing brown hair and sparkling blue eyes.

I'm not going to lie, but she was hot! It was love at first sight. I introduced myself to her and she couldn't stop smiling.

I knew that she was into me by how shy she was when she talked. I was so nervous to get to know her because I was just a skinny boy with no muscle or tan or anything and I didn't know what kind of person she was attracted to, but I tried to have confidence.

She was so cute I couldn't get over it. I finally asked her out to dinner on Friday night and she accepted. She took my phone out of my hand and put her number in it and said, "call me". My stomach dropped.

That was only the beginning. Norma and I had been together for almost ten months, and we were deeply in love until one day after school when it all almost ended.

I had always told her that I would be loyal, but she never believed me and she hasn't talked to me in days and I didn't know why.

She had left me these mean voicemails on my phone about how all guys are the same and she knew that I wouldn't be able to be tied down to one girl.

She was so mad over something that I had no idea about. She told me that she has clear evidence that I had been cheating with another girl.

She told me that over the past few days I had been acting weird and distant and she felt like things just weren't the same. I didn't know what she meant.

"I had my reasons for being distant" I had told her, "But I didn't cheat". She claims that there was a long brown hair lying on his computer, which couldn't have been hers because she had light blonde hair, and he didn't have a sister who could have been the owner either.

She also saw the flower store website up on my computer screen and knew that those couldn't be for her because there wasn't any holiday or anniversary coming up that they could be for her.

She wouldn't return my phone calls or texts or anything. I thought she was going to leave me for good and never wanted to talk to me again.

I couldn't handle that. I loved her so much. And I had done nothing wrong. Secretly, I had been out shopping for days to try to buy her a promise ring and flowers just because I loved her, and I wanted to surprise her.

I had gone out with her sister to try to find the right one. And she wouldn't even talk to me. I couldn't tell her the truth without ruining the surprise. I didn't know what to do.

I had an idea so that I might still surprise her. I called her mom while she was at work and told her the truth and the whole story behind why Norma and I haven't been talking.

We arranged for me to go in their house and surprise her my own way. I went in while everyone was at work and put a path of white rose petals all the way upstairs to her room.

I lit candles all around her room and put a dozen red roses and the ring in the box on her bed. I hid in her closet waiting for her to come home. I heard the door open and her frantically walk up the stairs.

I knew she had to be confused. She shot into her room and went over to the bed and started to tear up. I popped out of the closet and wrapped my arms around her.

I explained to her that that hair she found was her sister's because I took her with me to pick out her ring and that the flower website was for her. It was all for her. I was loyal and I didn't lie. It was all for the better of our relationship.

We finally were able to trust each other, and she started to not be so bothered by anything I was doing.

She used to completely blow up my phone every time I was out anywhere just to make sure I wasn't cheating on her or doing something that she wouldn't like. But we finally passed that, and everything was good.

Later, the following week, I was at home working on my homework to keep my grades up so that I could get into a good college, which is what my parents so desperately wanted. I needed to start being more efficient.

Norma knew I needed time to study and had a hair appointment at Glitz salon, just down the street from her house. She'll tell you the story from here.

I pulled up to the salon and I was five minutes early for my appointment, which excited me because I could have a sit down and read a magazine, which was one of my favorite parts.

I picked up the Glamour magazine from the top of the coffee table and opened it up to the middle. It was an ad for lip gloss of course. Right then I felt a soft breeze hit my face. I shivered a little, and a guy sat beside me. It was Josh, my ex-boyfriend and first love.

"Hi Norma! "He was a tall muscular guy with a nice tan and a gorgeous smile!

"Oh, hi Luis! How have you been?"

"I've been good how about you?"

"Great," We kept up with the small talk until my hairdresser called me back to the chair to get my hair done.

"Well, it's time for me to go back," I said.

"Oh, that's okay, maybe after our appointments we can get together for some lunch to catch up".

"Sounds good to me, I'll meet you at the café down the street in an hour". I walked back to the chair and sat down.

All I could think of was Luis and our past. How much fun we used to have, and how much I missed him every day.

Then Jake popped into my head. "How would Jake feel about this?" I knew that he trusted me, and I could get away with it without him even finding out that we went out to lunch. It wasn't a big deal.

Sitting there getting my hair cut and blow dried I had racing thoughts. Thoughts about what might happen, or where this lunch could go, and how to make sure Jake never found out about this.

I love him, but I love Luis too. I admit I still have some feelings for Josh, even though I convinced myself that I didn't. We had only broken up because his mom had died and he was too emotionally unstable to have a girlfriend, but he seemed to be doing okay now.

I wondered if this was some kind of sign, how he had popped back into my life. I took off my ring that Jake had given me and slipped it into my pocket.

After I left the salon, I quickly walked down the road into town where the café was. I didn't know if Josh was already there or not, but I sure didn't want to wait outside and risk the chance of someone seeing me and telling Jake, so I went inside.

Luis had already been seated in a little booth towards the back of the restaurant waiting for me. I sat down and right away we started talking like we hadn't even been apart. It was weird.

Luis and I had never talked like this. This was the best date I've ever been on. I felt so happy to finally see him again and catch up. He was the perfect guy. But I did feel bad about going behind Jake's back.

After lunch I had to go back home and start working on homework of my own. It was awkward trying to say goodbye because neither of us wanted to.

I felt these butterflies in my stomach that I used to get when he looked at me. He leaned in for what I thought was going to be an innocent hug and he kissed me. I felt my stomach drop and I kissed back.

He grabbed me and held me close. He told me that he missed me and wished we could be back together again. I started to tear up again.

Then suddenly I felt my phone in my pocket vibrate, it was Jake. I ignored it and slid it back in my pocket.

Back at home, Luis was concerned. "Why wouldn't she answer my calls?" I thought to myself. "She had to be out of the salon by now…"

I was starting to get worried because I was blowing up her phone and she still hadn't answered. Maybe I should go try to check up on her. I hoped that everything was okay. I walked down the road to the salon that she always went to and went inside.

The lady at the front desk said that she had left over an hour ago and said she was going to the café down the road for lunch. So, I left. I headed the other way down the road again and I saw her there on the sidewalk outside of the café.

I walked closer because I saw that she wasn't alone. She was kissing someone! I thought, "This couldn't be Norma, it must be someone else," I got closer and sure enough it was.

She cheated on me. She went behind my back and hooked up with another guy! So many thoughts and emotions were running through my head I didn't know what to say or what to do.

I could feel my whole body heating up and the sweat trickled down my neck.

Between breaths she looked up and saw me standing there. She turned away pretending to be someone else.

"How could you do this to me!" I turned and started to walk away, tears filling my eyes.

"It's not what it looks like, I'm sorry!" She ran after me.

"How could you do this to me? After all we've been through, after I bought you that ring! It was all a lie, you never loved me.

You are so fake!" I busted into tears and started to walk away. I took off the necklace that she bought me from Florida and threw it at her feet.

As it bounced off the sidewalk into the street and turned the other way. Right then I knew it was over. She was my life and now she was gone. My world was gone.

After months had passed full of sorrow and pain, I began to get over her. I started to move on and hang out with new people, new girls.

There wasn't any that I met that would ever match up to Norma, but eventually I knew that special girl would come along and make me completely forget about Norma.

Until then, I decided that there were more important things in life and that I had to live it up while I still had time.

My life wasn't over, I just came upon a rough patch and things finally were starting to smooth over. It wasn't the end of the world after all.

Chapter 30

Fresh as a Flower

The first thing I noticed as she sat down was her smell. It was so unique and beautiful that it left an everlasting imprint on my mind.

It was as if the freshest flowers all came into bloom at once. She sat next to me in Math class.

We were close enough for me to notice everything about her. Whether she wore her up or down or a sweatshirt or tee.

She was the most beautiful person I have ever laid eyes on. Everything about her was perfect. Her slightly curly light brown hair just brushed the crease on her lower back or her gorgeous deep brown eyes that seemed to penetrate everything they saw.

Her thin, fit frame from all the hours of working out left her with the body any boy could have wanted but didn't have.

I noticed everything she did like glance at me on the way to class or back track in my direction. Was hoping that one day she'll give me a hint that she liked me as well.

But for now, I'll sit near her, intoxicated with her smell, imagining she put it on for me. working up the courage to talk to her.

Chapter 31

The Werewolf

"I can't believe you'd have a child, then imprint on another woman!" my mother screeched. "I can't control it and I'm so sorry." Dad sighed.

She put me back on the ground but held me close. I was only five years old, and I loved my dad, but I was a mirror image of my mother.

My father was a werewolf, and his new girlfriend was someone I liked. "Sorry doesn't cut it; Rose we're leaving now." She hissed. I reached for my dad's arms, his eyes filled with pain, and he turned away.

"Daddy!" I cried as mom dragged me away; his arms reached for me, but it was too late.

Every year after that I wrote a letter to my father, but my mother always ripped it up. I was now seventeen and I was in so much pain because I wanted to see my father.

In such pain, that my father's werewolf genes turned me to a werewolf myself. "I will not have a freak in my house; get out of my site!" she screamed.

I burst from my clothes and ran out on four paws. I didn't need to bring clothes because I found clothing that changed when I changed.

I ran without looking back and laid under a tree. Sleeping peacefully, I didn't realize I was on vampire's land.

There was a low hiss and my eyes opened. I was on my feet and looking around. My blue eyes could not find the source of the sound, so I turned human.

"Who's there; I smell you." I growled. There was a small laugh and I started to run. I could hear someone following behind me, but my four legs were fast.

I did not stop until I was exhausted. "How funny, I won't get tired." A voice hissed. I let out a warning growl.

"Touchy, touchy, a lone little werewolf pup doesn't scare me; I'm just curious because you're a girl." He replied. I turned back to the human, and he laughed. "Why are stalking me?" I snarled.

"You smell really good for a werewolf, and I like wolves; they taste good." He taunted. I got up and ran on four paws. "I'm just as fast as you, but I'll catch up when you sleep." He called from next to me.

I ran all night until my paws ached and I collapsed on the ground. I was looking up to see my killers face when a chorus of growls erupted around me.

I saw the corner of his head and a flash of yellow before he disappeared. A pack of wolves surrounded me and started leading me toward the town.

"A stray werewolf girl, I wonder why I can hear her." One asked. "My name is Rosa, my dad was second in command for a pack of werewolves; his name was Eric?" I thought.

"You found the right pack, but you shouldn't be a wolf?" he asked again. "Well, I am now lead me to my father."

I commanded. I turned to human form and sighed. The tan colored one snorted and the other two laughed.

I was escorted to my father in a brisk walk. "Dad!" I cried as I ran toward him. "Rosey is that you?" he asked as I nodded, and he pulled me into a tight hug.

"I can't go back home dad; she won't take me back." I sobbed. Behind me a boy spoke. "She's a werewolf, Eric."

The boy spoke. "No, she isn't!" my father grimaced. I turned in a wolf and back. "My little girl has changed; I am so glad to have you in our pack."

My father smiled. "I know, dad, and I've missed you too much." I beamed. "Me too." He sighed. After our reunion I got to know the pack.

The alpha was Jay; he was the russet-colored wolf. Next is Chris; he is a tanned wolf. Sam is a brown wolf and Ben is a cream-colored wolf.

I was the different werewolf in human form and wolf form, strait brown hair in human form and grey hair in wolf form.

They all had black eyes, but I had blue eyes. "Rosa, do you remember Alice?" My mother called, and I nodded. "Rose, I've missed you." She blushed and I ran to hug her.

I had always wished she were my real mom. "I've missed you too, Alice." I answered. Behind me Jared snorted, and the rest of the pack laughed. I ignored them and smiled at Alice. The pack is my family now; they are my brothers and I their sister.

I had finally settled into new habits of patrol because of my little vampire friend, when Ben reported that the leech was trying to find his way in.

I raced toward where he was, and I heard footsteps of the others coming to Ben's aid. I was just about to leap when the bloodsucker's eyes met mine.

Everything that held me down disappeared because he held me there now. "Rosalynn, he's a freaking leech!" Jared pointed out, but I could not look away from his topaz eyes that held mine.

"I've been trying to get through your bodyguard to apologize." He smiled. I took a small step forward toward my "supposed" enemy. In the minds of the other wolves, he smelled awful, but to me he didn't.

"She's going to get herself killed; at least after he kills her, we can kill the leech." Someone behind me whispered in his mind.

I drop the vampire's gaze and growl at the brown wolf. I turned back to his topaz eyes and his perfect lips were carved up in a smile.

I took another step, and he held out his hand. I turned human and placed my hand in his. "Sorry, they aren't my bodyguards, I'm part of this pack." I beamed.

"Would you accept my apology?" he asked, and I nodded. "Thank-you miss, my name is Jesse." He informed. "My name is Rosa." I answered.

His hand felt cold in mine, but I liked it. We stared into each other's eyes for a moment until there was a painful whimper behind us.

"They want to go, and they aren't going to leave without me." I sighed painfully. "Go before their noses start bleeding, I imagine I don't smell too good to them; will I see you again?" he asked, and his eyes pleaded.

All I could do was nod, but I knew I'd have to sneak out. I gave him one last smile before I turned around and changed back to a wolf.

I ignored their thoughts and ran back home. I changed back at home, and I waited for the others to gain up on me.

I had made them some of the clothes that didn't rip when you transformed, but that transformed with you. "What the heck was that Rosa?" Jared yelled.

We were outside my house and my dad came out. "I can't control who I imprint on, Jared!" I snapped. "She imprinted?" my dad asked. "Yes, why don't you tell him what you imprinted on?" Jared growled and my father's gaze landed on me.

"His name is Jesse and he's a vampire." I whispered as I looked down. "Jared, if my daughter has imprinted then you need to trust her judgment, not yours because it would hurt the whole pack if you killed him."

My father said calmly. I looked up and was about to ask what he meant, but my eyes landed on Jared's face. His face was distorted by sorrow and lost. "Jared, please, let me see him again; that's all I ask of you." I pleaded.

"Sure, why not; go love your leech, but I don't care if I see you again." He snapped as he turned and changed. I changed and followed him.

In my mind I saw his thoughts. I saw myself in his eyes as he tried to understand me. Something clicked together in my own head. "You were hoping to imprint on me?" I whispered lightly. "Yes, look I'm sorry I yelled, but do you really love him?" he sighed.

"Yes, more than I could ever love someone else." I admitted. "Then I won't yell or scream, you can see him whenever." His thoughts were kind and I grinned. "You will always be my favorite brother, but then again if they heard that you're all my favorite brothers." I teased. "You're still my favorite sister." He beamed. I turned and ran back to where I knew I would see him.

"Jesse, where are you?" I asked in my human form. "Up here!" he called. I looked up to see him on the edge of branch in the tree. I was reaching toward a branch to climb up when he was suddenly behind me.

"Let me help, I don't want you falling out of a tree." He sighed and I nodded. He grabbed me and slung me over his shoulder. Then he climbed up the tree, ran up the tree more accurately and placed me on the branch. I gasped at the view, and then smiled at Jesse. "In the others' mind you smell like bleach, but to me you don't; is it the same with you?" I breathed.

"You smell different than the others, kind of like cinnamon rather than wet dog." He beamed. "I wonder why that is?" I pondered aloud.

"Maybe it's because of the connection between us." He offered. "In our pack, we call that connection imprinting and it's kind of rare." I informed.

"The russet-colored wolf looked kind of mad when your eyes met mine, was he mad because I'm a vampire?" Jesse whispered.

"Yes and no; he wanted to imprint on me." I sighed. "You would be better off imprinting on him." He muttered.

"Don't say that he's like my brother and I love you!" I hissed. "You really don't care that we're mortal enemies?" he asked. "I wouldn't care if you drank human blood, but you don't, and your personality is all I care about."

I explained and he surprised me. He turned and wrapped his arms around me. "You are the most wonderful being I've ever met."

He laughed and I leaned into him. "I get that from my dad." I teased. When we sat together on that branch, I realized something. I was finally whole because he is my other half.

Something else occurred to me while sitting there, it would be easy from him to kill me if he decided to, but I knew he never would even think that.

"Would you like to meet my family?" he asked. "Um, sure, but would they be okay with the whole mortal enemies thing?" I pointed out.

"Bella and Zachary are fine with that part; they're my brother and sister." He explained. "Then, I'd love to meet them." I beamed. He scooped me up in his arms and jumped down from the tree.

I expected him to put me down, but he started to run, and I laughed. When he stopped, he gently put me down and I stood closer to him. I wasn't afraid of going into the house of vampires, but they aren't going to like me.

The place we stopped at was a beautiful home. "Claire, Zachary, are you guys home?" he asked when we walked inside. Standing in the doorway I saw a female and a male staring at me.

"Jesse, a little warning before you bring the pup home." The male that could only be Zachary sighed and Claire hissed at him. Jesse stiffened beside me.

"Hello, Rosa, please, pardon my husband's manners; we're glad to finally meet you." She beamed. "It's nice to meet you too." I blushed and next to me, Jesse relaxed. "Sorry Rose, I am really glad to meet you too." Zachary grinned.

I smiled at him, and his grin grew. "Claire has a talent to predict the future, just like I can see threw another person's eyes." Zachary informed.

"Really, I can play the flute." I laughed. "Don't worry, Rose, I can't do anything either." Jesse teased.

"Well, truthfully, you both have a weird talent." Claire pointed out and we stared at her. "You can love each other without conflict or the wet dog smell; sorry, but when you're together you smell good."

She smiled apologetically. "I would take that over anything." Jesse blurted. "So, would I; it would really suck if we were always trying to kill each other.

I agreed and there was a pause. "You know I've never seen a werewolf with blue eyes." Claire announced. "My mother wasn't part of the tribe and I look exactly like her, but my dad was in the tribe." I explained.

"So, you got your wolf traits from your dad." Zachary pondered and I nodded. "I like werewolves now, they're so cool." Zachary teased.

"Zachary, did you use your talent on our new friend!" Claire scowled. "I don't mind, and vampires are cool, well, at least you guys are." I laughed. "Well, it's time for me to return you home before they send out a search party." Jesse frowned and grabbed my hand.

"Wait, Claire will I get to see you guys again?" I asked and she closed her eyes. "Yep, tomorrow." She laughed and we all joined in. "then, I guess I'll see you tomorrow!" I called as Jesse walked me out the door.

"They like you too." He smiled. "I know; I wish you could meet my family, but they really hate vampires." I frowned. He stopped and turned to me. I looked up into his eyes and smiled. "I love you, Rose, and I wish I could be a werewolf too." He sighed.

"I love you too, but I love you the way you are." I corrected. "Really?" he asked as he pulled me closer. I could see the humor in his eyes. "Ye…" I started but broke off when his lips met mine. We stood there for a moment then we broke off.

"You are my world now." He whispered against my lips and then he kissed my forehead softly. I leaned up to kiss his forehead and then I wrapped my arms around him. His arms automatically wrapped around me and held me close.

"Your pack is coming." He sighed. "I wish I didn't have to leave." I frowned. "Maybe someday you won't have to."

He started and kissed me one last time. "See you tomorrow!" I called to him as he disappeared and then I changed to my wolf form. "You don't have to send bodyguards."

I thought. "Sorry, we were worried about you." Chris called. "Yah, we missed our little sister." Sam teased. "I missed you too, you little brats." I laughed. "I'm not a brat." Ben whimpered.

"Oh, Ben, you know you are!" I snorted and we laughed. "Rosalynn, welcome home." Jared called. "Jared, thank-you for understanding."

I sighed and everyone, but Jared and I groaned. "You like her, Jared!" Sam teased. "Sam, don't you like Stacey?" he growled.

After that Sam was quiet and we walked back home in human form. "You got to meet his family, when do we get to meet him?" Jared asked. "Oh, yah, well I thought you wouldn't be okay with that." I rushed.

"You hurt my feelings, just kidding, he's a part of our family now, so we might as well meet each other." He grimaced. I ran over and gave him a small hug.

"You are the best brother a girl could have!" I laughed. "Can't breathe!" he teased. We walked home in silence and my dad was thrilled to hear the news. I went to bed filled with happiness.

In the morning I broke the good news to Jesse. He picked me up and twirled me around. "We can be together forever if this works." He smiled. "Either way I'll stay by your side." I reminded him.

"I know, but I want you to stay with your family." He admitted, but he kissed me before I could respond. "That's not fair when you do that." I teased. "What kissing you is unfair?" he beamed.

"No, you are kissing me when…" but I got cut off again as he kissed me. "I give up!" I laughed and then I kissed him. "I didn't need to see that!" Zachary called.

"Claire, Zachary!" I grinned. Jesse wrapped his arms around me, trapping me close to him. "Rose, we saw the good news!" Claire laughed. "Jess, are you okay going to meet a bunch of wolves by yourself?" Zach teased.

"If anything goes wrong, I'll defend him with tooth and claw, but our alpha had this plan so nothing's going to happen." I smirked.

"I'll survive and I like werewolves." He said as he held me tighter. "I do too, so don't mess this up." Zachary said as he looked at me. I knew he liked me as a little sister.

"Zachary, if anyone is going to mess this up it'll be you and your big mouth." Jesse taunted and let go of me.

"Oh, dear a sissy vampire is picking on me; come taste my skills." Zachary hissed. "Claire watch Rose so she doesn't get hurt while I teach your husband manners." Jesse ordered. Claire chuckled and pulled me across the clearing to watch. "Do they always pick on each other?" I laughed.

"Yeah, but Zach's been teasing Jesse for his lovey-dovey nonsense when he's around you." She explained. I watched Zachary lung at Jesse and miss. "Zach's fast, but Jesse's faster." She followed my gaze. "Rose, watch me and I'll show you how a real vampire fight." Zach called.

He didn't see Jesse pounce and got pinned down. "Don't listen to him, he's always wrong!" Jesse flashed a smile and unpinned Zachary. "I am right sometimes!" he smiled. Jesse appeared at my side in a split second.

"You're really good at fighting." I commented and Zachary frowned, "you're good too." "About time someone recognizes my talents." Zachary muttered while grinning at Claire.

She walked gracefully over to him, and they kissed. Jesse pulled me into a hug, and we watched Claire fight against Zachary. Zachary raced at Clair, but she moved out of the way before he came close.

She jumped and landed on his back with her teeth at his throat. "I always win." She smiled as she kissed his throat. "Would you like to try?" Jesse whispered in my ear, and I nodded. "Zachary, let's see if my girlfriend can kick your butt too."

He teased. "You're on pup." He grinned at me, and I gulped. "Don't worry he won't hurt you." Jesse breathed only to me. I took my place in the clearing and Zachary lunged.

I dodged and transformed into a wolf. "Just having fun, in no danger." I thought to my brothers. "You will always be the crazy one." Jared responded.

Zachary came back running at full speed and I leaped up. I landed on his back and my teeth at his throat. I turned back while still on his back.

"You'll win someday." I whispered in his ear. I jumped down and ran to Jesse. "See that was nothing!" Jesse smiled. "Clair, will you fight me?" Zachary asked and she nodded. "How about girls against the guys?" I suggested and they nodded.

I took my place next to Claire and faced the other two. The boys lunged and I dodged effortlessly. "Is that all you got?" I asked Jesse. "You wish." He smirked.

He ran around me until he was a little blurry, then I jumped up when he leaped. I landed on top of him, but he threw me off.

Next thing I knew he had his arms around me and was kissing my throat. "Cheater!" I laughed. In the clearing Zachary had Claire in the same hold. "What was that early about you always winning?" he purred.

"You always win." She laughed. We sat in the clearing for a while thinking. "That was fun, let's do that again sometime." I yawned. "You must be tired."

He whispered. "A little, but I don't want to leave." I answered. "Come on sleepy head, I'm taking you home." He grinned and he cradled me in his arms. As he ran, I fell asleep in his arms. "Wake-up, Rose, you need to go home." Jesse ordered.

"I think she's exhausted, why don't you carry her home." Jared called. Why were Jared and Jesse together? "Okay, is it if I stay; I don't want her to freak out." Jesse answered and Jared nodded. Last thing I was aware of was, his cold arms around me.

I woke up in the morning and smiled when I saw him. "You're very peaceful when you sleep." He sighed.

"I would say the same, but you can't sleep." I smiled. "Well, everyone approves of us, and you slept through it all." He announced.

"Really, we can be together?" I gasped and he nodded. I threw my arms around him, and he kissed me.

"Let's go get some breakfast, I believe Claire is making something." He grinned. "Okay." I beamed. He slung me over his shoulder and ran out into the forest. "Rose, do you like pancakes?"

Claire asked and I nodded. I ate and their eyes followed my every movement. "I think I need to go help my pack, but I'll come back later." I frowned.

"Come back for dinner and you can have a sleep over with Claire while we hunt." Jesse agreed and I nodded. I turned to a wolf and ran toward my awaiting pack. "I'm sorry I've left." I apologized.

"It's okay, we want you to be happy." They all responded at once. "What does that mean?" I thought. "It means you don't have to worry about the tribe, go follow your heart and we'll call if we need help." Jared sighed.

"You guys don't want me?" I grimaced. "Of course, we want you sis, but go enjoy your life." Jared grinned. "I love you, brothers." I smiled. "We love you too, sister." Chris grinned.

I did a few laps on the border and got ready for dinner. I wore a long red dress and curled my hair. I grabbed some stuff to bring over. There was a knock on the door, and I threw it open. He smiled at me, and then kissed the top of my head. "Rosalynn have fun."

My father called. Jesse scooped me up and ran to his house. "You look stunning, Rose." He complemented. "Thanks, you look amazing." I admitted. We walked inside and I saw the other two lying away in the kitchen.

"Are you making them cook?" I asked. "They love cooking, but there's nobody to cook for until now."

He laughed. "Dinner will be ready in ten minutes, why don't you get her stuff set up?" Claire called. He scooped me up again and ran upstairs. "This is my room, but since I don't sleep, you can use it." He joked. "I'll share." I beamed.

He made the bed and I put my bag in the closet. "That's a pretty color on the wall." I blurted. His walls were green like the outside.

"Dinner's ready!" Zachary called just when Jesse was going to answer. We walked downstairs and sat down.

"Thank-you for making this, Claire, Zachary." I smiled. They made chicken with some rice and asparagus.

Once I had eaten everything, I noticed the others left. "Jesse, were did they…" I started, but he stopped me. "Please promise not to laugh, but Rosa, will you marry me?" he asked, and I froze.

"Yes!" I squeaked. In the other room I heard laughter, but there was additional laughter than normal.

Jesse walked me in, and my pack was in the room too. "Surprise, Rose, we came to wish you good luck and that you have happy days." Jared grinned. I ran and hugged each person.

"You guys are the best." I called to everybody. "Your father sent his blessings too." Sam informed and I nodded. When everyone left, I went upstairs and laid down on the bed.

"Good night and sweet dreams." Jesse whispered. I fell asleep in his arms. We planned the wedding, which is in a week, and made invitations.

"You look beautiful." Claire called as she was adjusting the dress. "I can't believe I'm going to be Mrs. Lupus in just a few minutes." I whispered. Lupus was Jesse last name.

"Yeah, it's really funny because Lupus in Greek means wolf." Claire informed. "That's weird." I smiled. She put on her brides' maid dress and Alice was already in hers.

"Okay, we're on." Alice announced and I hear music in the background. My father stepped up to me and escorted me down the aisle.

Lupus's backyard was covered with white and red roses. There was also a chain decorated with bows and ribbons lining the aisle. Jesse looked remarkable in black.

The preacher prattled on, and I almost kissed Jesse before he said, "you may kiss the bride." "Before I join these two does anyone object?" the preacher asked. "Yes, I do; Rose you're just going to break his heart when you are freaking imprint on his best friend!" a familiar voice shouted.

"Mother!" I gasped. "I'm taking you home so you can't hurt that poor man." She snapped. "I imprinted on him mom, and I don't want to live with you!" I growled. "I don't care young lady!" she snarled as she grabbed my arm and tried to move me.

"Don't you understand, I have always disliked you; I like father more." I admitted and her eyes filled with sorrow. "Go home and leave us alone; you've just ruined my wedding." I burst into tears as I ran into the house.

Jesse followed me but stopped to glare at my mother. "Rosey, it's okay." He whispered as he held me against his chest. "She...had to come...today."

I sobbed and he stroked my hair. "Let's go back outside and finish this; then I'll take you to a little waterfall I found." He reasoned and I nodded. He walked me back and we finished the wedding.

He kept his promise and took me to the waterfall. My immortal friends came too, along with Alice and my dad.

My mom left, after cursing at my father. "Hello, Mrs. Lupus." He laughed as we swayed back and forth.

"We made it; a vampire and a werewolf got married." I smiled. "The beginning of change." He added. "You own my imprinted heart." I beamed.

"You own mine too." He smiled. He leaned down, I froze where I stood, and we kissed. Our lives are intertwined with fate and romance.

Chapter 32

The Heartbeat

I want a man in him. Still. But that's nothing the heart can't take into its gentle shaping hands of sandpaper. Rough, yet prepared to handle with care.

Leaving minuscule scratches on the glass frame surrounding the orb of love, which has been freely given to him. Given to Stay.

Once taken it can never be given back whole. From which the sell is derived. It desires to be accepted, not stolen. The short-lived loves that exercise the hands give sell to one of the special designated.

The joy that fills your spirit is with Stay. Until he gives back what he stole or took he will keep that joy. If it's back and forward, he may give it back. If not, he will keep it forever. Possibly until you are released.

Stay should care. He should be amazed. But he said, "don't go". My mind pushed his words into "stay gone".

The words transformed in front of my eyes. Turned Around. Seeing him and my sigh. They say, "let the heart take control; not the mind". My mind is speaking in yelling tones. My heart in a faint whisper. How will I know when my heart collides?

When I feel his heartbeat dancing with mine. The spots of shine on his face alarm me. Stay was always so damn dark. Depressed.

Only because of that pole sticking out of his chest. Keeping me away. No matter what I do, Stay will never be the way. I wish it was so, but he's just. Nothing. Not in the manner of the law, but he is just.

My heart pounds thinking about him. I wish Stay was here next to me. But with my mind in yelling tones, he is wary and stays away. That pole doesn't help. His sun shines in clicks and bangs.

When he turns round and hits that pole against something conscious. My sun no longer shines. Stay stole my sunlight.

Stacked bodies of love cover my view of the outer. My view of the frozen. As much as Stay lies to himself…

He is broken. I am no longer reflective. Together we broke the mirror of self-righteousness.

Now you may ask why my sun doesn't shine. Because Stay didn't give it a chance. It was up to him. Only Him.

Ever since I opened my eyes to the world. I hoped he would too, but how could he when I had but one eye free. I want him to call me back to him. Why the negative? I just want that warm, red, love.

Every day away from what is to be held close makes me want to stay more and more. His glimmering smile, or his passing glance do as much damage as they do repair.

Seeing his hand run down her shins. The stops that took a day to conspire. One day free. Need. Whorish need. Don't trust a ho. Especially when packing such enormous blue fire.

The best course of action is to stay alone. The tears that bleed the page will only make you stronger. Staying will make you stronger.

The constant thought that, unearthly he is incredibly close. Who but him knows how earthly close. Why can't I know? Why can't it be both what I want and what's good for me? All things go.

Where does this backward heart of glass go? The fake smiles that embody the subtle hatred of Stay sears. Why? The subjective answers empty off into the distant void. And you won't love.

I wished it all would bend. But he still governs my every waking breath. Like a tidal wave that never breaks, I will run and run and never Stay.

There's no way back that I could face. As much as I hate it, no one will ever take Stay's place. The artifact of love is a complexity; too sweet, too bitter, too much, too little. A fleeting emotion derived from a notion that people can actually care for each other.

Staying is a wonderful wonder. I can't feel it right now across the room. But a world apart. Our eyes meet for a moment, and the feelings start.

Pouring into my veins, down to my fingertips. My hair slips, breaking the connection. But through all this chaos I still feel the direction of Stay's eyes pointed directly towards mine. He stayed trying to break through the invisible wall between us two.

> "I must leave soon, dear.
> Away from you I do fear.
> I give you my heart,
> Sealed with a tear.
> A precious package.
> Handle with care.
> Do you miss me my love,
> from away over there?"

Stay's small sins prevent him from their words. The wavering notes filter through my emotional fall. If only I had a voice. You can't sing through a straw.

The right time came, and he was what I grew to hate. He can stay if he wants to. We knew I wanted him to stay, but why not me? What have I done? What have I not done? They all require one answer.

Please stay. Oh, please stay. When you walk away you don't hear me say "please, oh baby, don't go". Simple and clean, it's hard to let go.

"Hold me. Whatever lies beyond this morning is a little later". Regardless of warnings, the future doesn't scare me at all. Nothing's like before when you walk away.

Stay, you don't scare me. Simple and clean as the way that you make me feel. For the moment your eyes open and mine close.

We both know your lonely road, but YOU chose it. I'm still right here waiting, Stay. All the things I ever wanted to know.

Morning comes and you don't want to know me anymore. Keep running Stay. Don't forget the inevitable, though. No matter where you go, it'll find you. It's like a bird. An eagle. While you and I sit, penguins.

You're beautiful, and that's for sure. You'll never fade. You're lovely, but I'm not sure. I won't ever change.

My love is great, my love is true. Rows of standard, our standard. Of course, Stay changed an ever-changing luminescent spirit of the sun.

I don't know where my soul is. Stay does, so you tell me why he won't tell me? He is the keeper of my most intimate pensive.

I fear for my dignity every moment because he could reveal me at any whim. Stay bewitched my body and soul. He started by looking at the glass of war.

You see what I want to see. So does Stay. It's MY looking glass after all. It's the only thing that I can control. To sit there and think that you're all right. You'll be wrong every time. And when I try to tell you…

I'm mad I'm laughing at Stay's pain. My scroll of seduction worked against me. I pressed my luck with Stay.

I think about him. But does he think about me? I'll never be satisfied even if he does. Because I want it all.

I want him to want me and to be with me. He wants me to be something else. It isn't like what we had at first. He thinks if he was in my life, I would have to accept him.

"Dear Stranger,

I'm writing this letter and I don't know your name. But I wanted you to know me. I hope that we can be… You still don't notice my love's direction with all this running through my mind. No matter how much I try I can't seem to find…you." Not Stay. No matter what I do. It will always be Stay. I want to love him. But I don't know if I can. Stay has broken my soul. And I have much less to give. You don't deserve the trouble I'll bring into your life. As much as I try, I don't feel worthy of your time. I live my life like tomorrow is your last, keep every moment special and try to love myself no matter what. I keep Stay close to my heart.

It is an irregularity. A gem in the place of time that repeats itself. From every soft crunching footstep against the future representing the past and the beauty of what could be.

A single tear of light shining through the panes of possibility. Remembrance of the different lengths of time in the eyes of the fake.

The gentle notes that rise and fall with the inept emotion of the conflicted souls who cry out to lonely ears. Grins show from ear to ear with the subtle change of a note.

I am a figment of his imagination. Pangs against the softened heart dissolve me. Barely visible, I cry out to the most unworthy for release. I cry for help.

The height pulls me up towards it. As low as I drop, I must always be saved and brought back to life, never happiness. Why is such evil pitted against me?

The twists and turns of that path confuse me. And when I am heard no more, with tears running down my face, I revel in the minute invisibility.

I force myself to be steadfast and make it through this dream that hinders me. And when my reality awakens, I will be remembered as a time of day. I will be naught but an explosion in the sky. The strange innocence that keeps me will fly off into the sunset.

If you float away, as least tell Stay to keep to the bottom of the hourglass. Let the sands of time trickle down the lines of your eyes.

At your best you are lust. What is love but a thought in your head. What is lust but a glimpse in your heart. What is time but a beat in your heart?

Chapter 33

The Mystery

His shaded eyes cast an aura of mystery about him, and with the beat-up leather jacket one might pin him as "The bad boy" but Sky knew better.

It began with a glance, then a smile. Soon they were talking. His name was Emanuel, and he had a secret, one that would tear them apart.

Sky was pretty and popular so naturally they couldn't be together, but they were in love.

He wanted her so badly, sometimes he cried. She knew two things, He was "the one" and he would eventually become her undoing.

Every day he told himself he would tell her and yet every time he was about to, she sealed his lips with a flourish of kisses.

He had done it.

He had killed a man. he had killed Sky's brother three years earlier.

He battled with his inner voices, trying to silence the madness.

They were together always but the guilt still overcame him.

"Sky?" he asked one quiet night alone.

She turned to him and said "yeah?"

He took a breath and let the story unfold itself.

Sky stood shocked.

The only sound in the room came from the distant ringing of Emmanuel's Cell phone.

"Sky?" Emmanuel pulled his shirt on.

"I am sorry I didn't tell you sooner"

She simply sat back on the bed and said "Just go Emmanuel"...

Something deep in his heart snapped and he knew this would be the last time he ever saw Sky.

"Baby, I love you and I am so sorry.

He leaned over and kissed her softly and tasted her pain and tears.

That night Emmanuel stared at the swirling water below him, as Sky had her final conversation with a knife.

Last breaths, lost love, love made, love found, Tears shed.

Searing pain and desperate pleas.

Want.

Love.

and Death are what and who Sky and Emmet are.

peace.

Chapter 34

Frustration

Back then, he was so sweet, a beautiful soul untouched by the filthy hands of man. But now, your aura foggy, your heart numb, you seem afraid to let yourself remember anything good we ever had.

She sighed, a long weary sigh. He'll never forgive her, and she doesn't need him to, after all he hasn't changed one bit.

Headphones blaring, she walks home alone, again. Crunch, crunch, the sound of one person's footsteps in the snow of last night is getting old.

I tried to hold your hand, but you'd rather hold your bitterness. She walks past one of many memories packed places, and sighs yet another sigh.

Who I am hates who I've been and who I am will take the second chance you gave me. Can't they find something else to sing about?

She trails along, her mind expressed clearly across her flushed face. Her mousy brown hair was nearly white with snowflakes; she was freezing. Stressed and in a hurry. She had left her winter jacket in her locker.

Frustrated as ever, the most average girl you've ever seen, with her nowhere near spectacular hair, with one colored streak, and her plain old brown eyes, and yet she still holds her head high and takes long confident steps, nearly home again.

Eyes brimming with tears, she thinks about the summer past. In her mind, she wants to say time wasted, but she could never regret that boy.

James, a challenge she took. In the process, she lost hope, trust, and the best friend she ever had.

She gained so much more it seemed; she gained trust for men, true love, and a great friendship. Nearly sixth months, half a year ago, she was the saddest person in the world.

Then he rescued her, in arms of man, she was safe for the moment, but soon to be doomed. Graciously, she accepted his offer of love and friendship, not once thinking of the people she was losing.

They were happy for so long, until her previous boyfriend jumped into the picture. He was finally willing to take her back after she waited for so long. She was committed to James; she was going to make things work.

She had to forget this troubled boy, she told herself,

"It didn't work the first time, why should it the second?"

In her head, she thought she could have both a relationship with James and a friendship with William, but reality quickly changed her mind. She wanted William with such intensity; it was excruciating.

She knew something different had to happen; he wanted her, and in turn she wanted him. She had William over to prove to herself and the world that she had self-control.

She just wanted to trust herself. She thought she could do it. Repeatedly she worked it out in her head, detail by detail, in the same fashion a weaver weaves a blanket. It happened, the exact opposite of what she had planned.

She was so lost, so confused. He kissed her; all she felt in her stomach was confusion. The entire night was a blur, as if she was on a roller coaster going ten-thousand miles an hour. She felt loved.

It was the first time in a long time that she felt that feeling. She was afraid of feeling affection, so she ran. In a non-literal sense, but she ran far away from anything that appeared safe inside her head.

It takes two people to kiss; she felt so guilty. James asked her if she was okay, and if she was hiding things, she could tell him with the assurance of love. No, she couldn't, but he didn't know the extent of the wrongdoing.

She thought she loved him. In her heart, mind, and soul, she wanted to keep what they had. Something in her though…had told her that it needed to end. And end it did.

It was viciously ripped from her worn hands, the only thing she knew. A blow in which she'd expected never to recover, but with William behind her, she felt invincible.

Will was always there to catch her when she stumbled. Thick or thin, he tried to help. When it seemed everyone's, souls were sick, their minds tainted with hatred, he always seemed to glow.

A shine so bright she couldn't look away. She didn't deserve him; he was her everything. His blonde hair, tousled every morning by her fingers, was the first she saw in a crowd. His blue eyes were so bright they could light up the world, and hers they did. She promised herself once never to love the same person twice, a promise meant to be broken. She gave up what she knew for one single soul. Rumors spread like wildfire throughout school, a rampage of lies. A textbook, dramatic, soap opera, rumor-filled life.

After he left, she was so alone. Even when she was with other people, there was an intense emptiness.

"I love you Marie, please don't let me go," James had told her so many times. "I love you too, James." she had said back. The words didn't belong to her, especially about him, she felt so shallow.

She lied every day of her life, for more than five months. She thought that if she kept saying and telling herself it was true, she would come to love him.

She knew it was impossible for her to love someone so close, when the one she wanted was waiting so far away. That night came back to her in dreams, blurry but ever so real, various times after that day.

A blaring noise had awakened her from her daydream. A long, drawn-out squeal from a car horn in front of her. Tires screeching, the sound of metal scraping across newly formed ice was deafening in both her ears.

Then there was an immense silence, a silence so awkward she could no longer keep her eyes shut. She was alive, but in front of her was the worst scene she'd ever witnessed.

A blue Jeep, and a black Ford pick-up truck had met their end, right in front of her. The Jeep was totaled, the truck severely damaged.

Blood was slowly seeping into the snow around the Jeep, turning it the most awful shade of crimson red. Swing marks surrounded the very place she stood. Quietly, nervously she thought. 'Oh, what have I done?'

"Someone call 911!" a frantic voice behind her yelled. She glanced back and saw a pile-up of cars, bumper to bumper. Completely oblivious to her surroundings until now, she sat down and sobbed.

Sirens wailing, she couldn't see, for her eyes were blurred from tears. In the blue Jeep, a small women struggled out.

Hands first, she it made out, blood everywhere. The small woman with wiry black hair emerged slowly from the damage. Tears swept down her face in a rush and melted the soft, innocent pure white snow around her.

Assured that the woman was alive, she stood and ran as fast as her feet would humanly carry her to the black truck. He opened his door, slowly at first, and with a quick jerk, he whipped shards of glass onto the snow. He was tall, black haired with green eyes, a strongly built man.

He was scared, fear plastered to his face. Fear, a look she guessed didn't come to this man much she guessed, judging how odd it looked on him. Scared to death, they ran to the ambulance that the paramedics were piling the woman into.

They were sure she was dead. This was a new chapter of life unfolding; she had been too wrapped up in her own silly dramatic issues.

She caused a terrible car accident, killing possibly someone's mother, wife, daughter, and friend, she took all the blame.

A life spent afraid of death, had caused a harsh reality. What was next in store, she could only imagine.

Chapter 35

Feelings

Eliezer pretended like he didn't care too much. However, I knew he was upset by my news. So upset he had to turn away from me so I couldn't see his tears.

I knew he was crying though. I know how he feels, even though he would never admit it.

I might sound like a horrible person to you right now, but to tell you the truth, it was a test. I don't like Sammy, I never have. I try not to throw up just thinking about seeing him again. Brown hair, gorgeous blue eyes, kind smile.

It doesn't sound so bad, does it? I guess I'm just crazy then. But hey, Sammy doesn't have the one thing I want: he's not Eliezer. He'll never be Eliezer. Case closed.

I ran around Eliezer to his front, grasped his shoulders with both hands, and looked him straight in the eyes.

His eyes, green like mine, hurt, but trying not to be. I tried not to get lost as I took a gulp of air.

His eyes.

"What do you think of Sammy? I mean, I care, I really care." I rubbed his shoulder as a sign of my words.

He just shook his head, his brown- blond hair falling in his face. Beautiful, perfect hair. It was dyed blond, but that didn't necessarily mean anything. It was still his hair. He flipped it out of his eyes, gently removing himself from my grasp as well.

His hair.

"He seems like a nice guy. I'm glad you have someone like I do." his lips tried to give a smile of encouragement, but his eyes still wouldn't hide their sorrow.

His lips, you could get lost in their words. I always did, every time I heard his voice. However, now I tried to control myself.

His lips.

I shrugged. "Thanks. How is Georgia?" I tried to sound offhanded, but I'm not a terribly good liar myself.

He looked at me like I tried to strangle him. "She's great. She's at a soccer game right now. I hope she wins." He stared off into the distance. I knew that he probably had no idea where she was.

I nodded. "That's good. Sammy's in Florida, surfing." I tried to sound like I wasn't trying to care. It wasn't working.

"He just left you here, all by yourself?" What did that look in his eyes, anger?

"No, I'm not alone. I have you, silly." Eliezer smiled. These were the words he wanted to hear. However, his voice, this time, expressed sadness.

"I just don't think that it's right for your guy to go surfing and not take you with him." "Your guy." He makes that sound so poisonous.

I laughed. "Oh, you know I don't like surfing." Besides, I thought, I don't really want to be around him at all. It's better that he's far, far away.

Eliezer looked at me, puzzled, and then looked around him. "Where's your roommate?"

I had to think for a moment. Remembering that we were in my cramped dorm room watching a movie was hard to recall.

I guessed that I really did get lost in his eyes again. Amazing how that happens, and I never realize it. That's not the way it is with Sammy. I'm looking for exit lights with that boy.

"Oh," I said offhandedly, "she's spending the weekend at her parent's house. I'm glad she's gone."

"You don't like your roommate?" Eliezer asked as he fell back into my bed, like he owned the place. He was here so often though, and it looked so natural.

All I wanted to do was fall into his arms and forget about Sammy and my roommate and school and this small room. However, I restrained. Why, oh why, did I restrain?

"It's not that I don't like her, it's just that this is our weekend. I don't like people disturbing the peace." I pulled my small TV set out of the closet and set it on the table.

"That's understandable. I like our alone time myself."

I laughed quietly. Of course, you do. Why won't you admit why? Having plugged the TV into a nearby socket and setting it on my desk, I went over to my collection of DVDs against the wall.

I had a large selection, almost as large as the number of books I kept in a shelf above my bed. What can I say? I like to read.

"What are you in the mood for?" I asked Jake as I searched for the perfect movie.

"Something frightening. I want some blood." Eliezer got up from the bed and came over to the corner where I was searching.

I poked his nose. "Do your selection preferences ever change?" He laughed. What a gorgeous smile.

"Not until I get my preference choice." He poked my nose back.

I laughed and shook my head. "I'm never in the mood for blood and guts, Deary. Pick something else." Eliezer smiled. He leaned over me, his head resting on my shoulder, and scanned the DVD titles with his forefinger.

How natural it felt to have him there. Did he notice the rightness of that position? Well, of course he did. He must have. That was too strong a feeling for me to share alone.

After a few seconds of careful searching, Jake tapped on a DVD with an orange and white cover. "Juno? I would expect you to pick something a little, newer."

He smiled. "I like this movie. Besides, it's only what, five years old? That's not much." He got up and walked over to the DVD player. I stayed down, paralyzed by our closeness.

"Five years can be a very long time, though. I mean, we've been best friends for five years. I consider that to be a very long time." I got up then, walked over to him, and made eye contact.

He nodded. "Yeah, you're right. In that sense, five years is almost forever." He smiled at me, but his eyes were unfocused. Perhaps mine were too. Perhaps we went back to the same day, a little less than five years ago. That first day at camp our second time around...

Chapter 36

El Almendro

If ever there was a place that could smell of desolation it was the hut in which this chronicle begins. The walls were made of terra cotta clay and were as pale as if a ghost had just brushed against them.

The wooden floor was cracked in many places like the life of the middle-aged man who sat gingerly on it. His hands were wrinkled, and his dexterous fingers busy whittling the piece of wood they now held with a chisel.

A shapeless figure began to appear out of the wood, a human form. The man's long tangled brown matted hair was flecked with bits of gray and would occasionally brush the figure.

Soon the figure was complete, and his adept hands moved the chisel to the face, a face worn from age, and loneliness.

Two green eyes filled with knowledge appeared first, then a broken nose, scraggly sideburns and finally the long beard. It was a likeness of him, and he felt proud.

He stood up and moved to the small three-legged table and got out a paint brush and painted 'Robert Lawrence' on the figure's back. Robert Lawrence himself was as melancholy and lonely as his surroundings.

Absent-mindedly he took the figure and carried it over to the sink. His hands let go of the figure and it sank into the basin of cold water.

A tear rolled down Lawrence's face and into his thick mustache his only solace in this forsaken place.

He wished now that he had never fled here to Nicaragua but had stayed in the states biting his tongue about the obvious indifference affecting the youth brought on by the technological age.

Once he'd been a Berkeley Professor of linguistics, but the monotony of life had gotten to him.

So, he'd resorted to a scheme he'd been planning for years, a fantasy to run away to a place hardly touched by civilization.

The Almendro province in Nicaragua was perfect. He'd faked his own death by drowning a mannequin of himself and escaping on the bottom of a cruise liner.

He was a widower; his wife had died when he was young in a terrible car accident. He never fully recovered from his loss and spent the next seventeen years whittling things out of wood.

When his classes were over, he would go to the forest, and find scraps of woodchips, and use them to carve his wife's name into the trees, until one day he found a piece of wood.

He took it home and bought a chisel and began working. Every day after classes it was always the same.

On campus he had become the linguistics professor who carved things out of wood. He didn't mind the loneliness then, because the whittling made him think of his wife and this gave him peace.

Somehow if he could ever carve her likeness out of the wood block before him, it would come to life, and he would be with her again.

Lawrence sighed and slipped out of his trance. Life was not simple. Those who worked hardest often did not receive their reward, and those who were lazy often stole more than was theirs.

Lawrence was a master of two Baltic languages, three romance languages and yet no words could describe how much he had loved that woman.

She was like an angel sent down into his life. He'd been a shy athlete at Oxford where he had gone as a Rhodes Scholar, and she had helped him come out of his shell.

Not a day passed without him remembering the moment they'd met. Robert was just walking along the lawn looking up at the sky and thinking when he saw her.

She was the most beautiful creature he had ever seen. After a few minutes, he thought of a subject to speak to her of and headed over.

It was a romance like no other Robert was crazy for and she was crazy for him. Her name was Anne. Her family lived in Glasgow, and after they both graduated Robert sought her father's permission to marry her.

They got married, and although there were arguments, they loved each other more than life itself.

One day, Anne was driving home from work, and a drunk driver swerved in front of her. Robert was teaching a lecture when he found out.

It felt like a thousand-pound steel block had just smashed into his chest. That was the day Robert's spirit died.

Now he was just a ghost seeking his wife, by chiseling wood. Robert knew his life was far more meaningful, and that he should move on, but he never did.

He went to the window opening it and felt the cool night air whistle in. The night air soothed him and was almost like a salve for his inner wounds.

He looked out and saw the long black trunk and branches spreading up from it. It was a beautiful almond tree, El Almendro. Before Robert died, he would carve his wife from it.

Chapter 37

Not Enough

It tingled my nerves, and it burned my flesh out. It made my heart pound as if my body had no end and it made me feel as miserable as no one could ever feel.

Why, for crying out loud, did I ever have the unfortune to experience a feeling that was not even accepted by my own health?

Well, you heard right, for it did. It did in such an awful way that it was impossible not to feel the pain.

Wise men say that emotional losses or personal problems are healed as time passes by. But to me, the fact of having lost this relationship would not heal over time.

In fact, it would get worse, because you figure out that every second, every minute gone is a period which you will not be able to experience again for it is a minute gone.

The massive amount of those minutes makes you realize, sooner or later, that the thing you have lost is vital, essential, and that without it, you will not only feel miserable, but you will die miserable for you will carry to your grave the weight of your conscience and the everlasting pain for having lost a crucial gap in your life.

All these thoughts were threatening me day by day. But only the power of my greatness gave me the strength to decide that I would not let myself be drowned by them.

I tried to convince myself that I was stronger than that. I kept repeating repeatedly that I did not need someone else to be happy, that I had to be satisfied with what was left of me.

After all, who needed that indescribable feeling that made my stomach hurt and my life nothing but unhappy? ... Well... I did. Who was I kidding? I needed to feel miserable.

I HAD to feel miserable, at least one more time. The time I had logged in that relationship was not enough.

I would never get enough of it for it was the most marvelous feeling I have ever had the privilege to experience.

Now here I was, lying in my bed, staring at a horizon that never grew closer and panicking over some guy who I was crying over for.

Tears streamed down for him as I gripped my guitar and crashed it against the wall. For a moment I thought he did not deserve me, and no guy had the right to mistreat me this way.

But minutes later I thought my bass would look good when suffering the same fate my guitar had suffered and that was when I considered paying for psychotherapy, though I did not.

Every damn night I kept thinking to myself these kinds of things, trying to understand why it was so not possible to have a perfect life, at least as far as love is concerned.

It was one of those nights when I heard some strange noises downstairs, which by common sense, I guessed were product of my insanity. But they were not.

Those noises were as real as my own pain. Someone was knocking at my door and the moment I opened it I had a short meeting with fate, or maybe luck. There he was, standing firm, arms opened, and he gave me the sort of look you get from a baby willing for a candy.

My mind was blank but somehow, I was filled with forgiveness, and I asked him over for a cup of tea.

About the Author

Norma Iris Pagan Morales was born in Ponce, Puerto Rico. Her parents, Juan Jose Pagan Rodriguez, and Digna Morales Figueroa, now deceased, always helped her with her projects as a writer and teaching career.

Norma had three siblings, Adelin Milagros Pagan Morales, Juan Jose Pagan Morales, and Julio Manuel Pagan Morales. Julio Manuel Pagan Morales died on September 19, 1998. He was also known for his writing / composer skills.

On February 17, 2023, Adelin Milagros Pagan Morales, her sister, died in the City of New York

Norma did all her academic studies in New York City, Puerto Rico, and Canada. She worked in the City of New York Police Department where she oversaw the full investigation of every new civilian and uniform member of the department.

As an Educator, she worked in New York City Bd. of Education, in Puerto Rico Bd. of Education as an English teacher. She also worked for the Puerto Rico Army National as an English Teacher.

She has teaching certifications for English as a Second Language and Teaching English as a Foreign Language. She also has teaching licenses to teach the following:

1. English Literature
2. Spanish Literature
3. Communication Skills in both English and Spanish
4. Office Procedures= These classes consisted of basic filing to writing memorandums and full company or organization reports.
5. Computers - Certified to teach Long Distance Learning

She has published 12 books: Proud of My Puerto Rican Bequest, Porque Soy Boricua? Poemas del Alma, Art in Written Form, A Baffling Short Stories Collection, On Job in the Big Apple, Nature's Rage in the Caribbean, You are the One, Unfaithful, Poemas Tiernos, Two Strangers, and Puerto Rican Soldiers Serving with Pride

www.ingramcontent.com/pod-product-compliance
Lightning Source LLC
Chambersburg PA
CBHW021643120626
46545CB00002B/685